Bags
the Modern Classics

✳ Clutches, Hobos, Satchels & More ✳

Sue Kim

Publisher: Amy Marson

Creative Director: Gailen Runge

Acquisitions Editor: Susanne Woods

Editor: Liz Aneloski

Technical Editors: Janice Wray and Gailen Runge

Cover Designer: Kristy Zacharias

Book Designer: April Mostek

Page Layout Artist: Casey Dukes

Production Coordinator: Jessica Jenkins

Production Editors: Julia Cianci and S. Michele Fry

Illustrator: Tim Manibusan

Photography by Christina Carty-Francis and Diane Pedersen of C&T Publishing, Inc., unless otherwise noted

Published by Stash Books, an imprint of C&T Publishing, Inc., P.O. Box 1456, Lafayette, CA 94549

Library of Congress Cataloging-in-Publication Data

Kim, Sue, 1969-

   Bags, the modern classics : clutches, hobos, satchels & more / Sue Kim.

      p. cm.

   ISBN 978-1-60705-388-0 (soft cover)

   1. Handbags. 2. Tote bags. 3. Sewing. 4. Fancy work. I. Title.

   TT667.K52 2011

   646.4'8--dc22

                          2011007725

Printed in China

10 9 8 7 6 5 4 3 2 1

{ contents }

{ acknowledgments }

If I were to describe the whole process of writing a book in one word, I would probably call it an adventure. During this adventure my biggest supporters were my husband, Jung, and our three lovely children—Chan, Caleb, and Veronica. They have always been here for me as my best friends and counselors. I also would like to thank June and Calvin, who have made numerous samples for me and have assisted in countless ways with this and other projects.

I express my thanks to the members of the C&T team who have helped with all the publishing-related business, especially Susanne and Liz. During the editing process, Janice supported me immensely. Thank you so much to everyone.

Thank you to Michael Miller Fabrics, Robert Kaufman Fabrics, and Amy Butler Designs for wonderful fabrics, and to Marvin and Julia of Miami Leather Company for supplying me with authentic Canadian leather. Also thanks to Michelle from Kallisti Quilts, who supported me with rare fabrics.

In addition to these people, I would like to thank my friends John, Sara, Aaron, Mary, Patrick, and Betty, who offer me endless support and help. Also, thanks to my family friends, Leo and JinSol.

Thank you, too, dear reader! May you enjoy many pleasant hours as you read and sew!

{ introduction }

The main function of bags and clutches is to hold and carry items; however, bags also provide a way for you to express yourself through fashion. That is why you spend time looking for the perfect bag—and why you're willing to pay more when you find it. Choosing a bag that represents your uniqueness is not an easy task, but it's a great excuse to shop . . . or sew a one-of-a-kind treasure.

This book will teach you how to make your own brand of handmade bags. Most of the bags use simple patterns, easy enough for the beginner. Note each project's level of difficulty before you begin. Levels of difficulty are explained on page 19. If you are a beginner, you can start by using the simpler patterns. Then, after you are familiar with the process of making bags, you can progress to bags involving more challenging techniques.

If you haven't made bags before, the projects might look complex, but if you follow the instructions one step at a time, you will realize that you need to learn only a few techniques to make beautiful one-of-a-kind bags. If you start with the simpler projects, you will gain confidence as you gain experience. Then the more complex projects will be easier to envision and to make. Don't expect to be able to produce extraordinary creations perfectly right from the start; expect rather to move through the learning stages, improving your skills with each bag. Having an open mind and setting the goal of finishing a simple bag is the first step. So don't be afraid—just jump into the wonderful world of making bags.

When I first started making bags, I had a hard time deciding which fabrics to use. Should I use this fabric or that one? One day, after watching me worry for quite awhile, a friend commented that in the time I spent worrying about which fabric to use, I probably could have made several bags. She was right. Now, rather than wasting my time worrying about a potential failure, I just make the bag. And if I am unhappy with the finished product, I choose a different combination of fabrics and try it again. This is a more efficient way of working, and I am able to make a lot more bags. It works for me, and I'm sure it will work for you. Fabric always looks more beautiful in the finished product than it does folded on the table. So don't be afraid to follow your instincts—just get started!

{sewing terminology}

Seam allowance

The area between the edges of the layered fabric and the line of stitching.

Straight stitch

A simple stitch and the most often used form of machine stitching.

Basting

Long hand or machine stitches used to temporarily hold two or more pieces together.

Backtacking

Backtacking is usually used to secure the beginning and ending of a line of machine stitching.

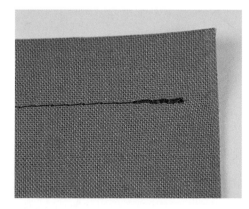

Sew a few machine stitches forward, sew a few stitches backward, and then sew forward to complete the line of stitching. At the end of the seam, sew a few stitches backward, and then sew forward to end the row of stitching.

Slip stitch

A type of stitching used to secure layers together almost invisibly by hiding the stitches between the layers. I prefer to use a double thread.

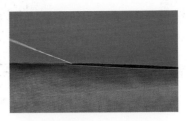

1. Thread a needle, and knot the end of the thread. Insert the needle into the fold of the fabric and pull the thread taut to hide the knot between the layers of fabric. (Use a thread color that matches your fabric—a shade darker will hide your stitches better.)

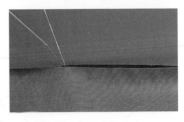

2. Insert the needle into the fold of the opposite layer of fabric, and pull the thread taut. Repeat as needed. Knot or secure with several stitches, and cut off the thread.

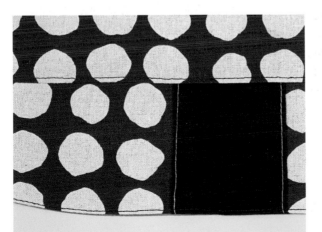

Top stitch

A line of machine stitching on the right side of the project. It is used for decorative purposes and also to press and reinforce the project. I like to use a fancy thread since it will show on the right side of the project.

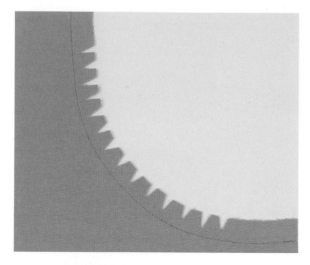

Clipping

Making small cuts on inner curves (concave seams) to help them lie flat when turned to the right side. Always clip within the seam allowance and never through the stitching.

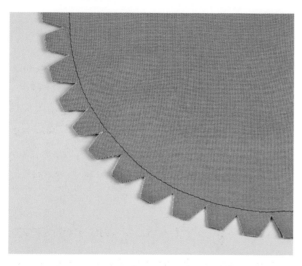

Notching

Removing small wedges of the seam allowance on outer curves (convex seams) to remove excess fabric, helping the seams lie flat when turned to the right side. Always notch within the seam allowance and never through the stitching.

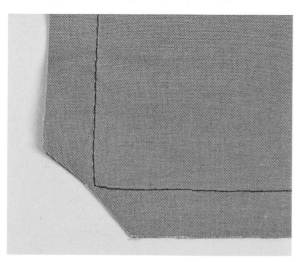

Trimming

Cutting away excess fabric in seam allowances to remove bulk, allowing seams and corners to lie flat.

{ useful information }

What Tools to Use

The main tools needed to make bags are a sewing machine and needles, scissors, pinking shears, a seam ripper, a ruler, marking pencils, and pins.

You don't need a fancy, high-end **sewing machine** to make the bags in this book. Two features to keep in mind when selecting a sewing machine: an easy-to-change bobbin and comfortable sewing-speed control.

The size of the **sewing machine needle** you use is based on the fabric and thread you choose. Refer to the instruction manual for your sewing machine for guidance.

When it comes to **scissors**, I recommend good-quality fabric scissors, which can easily be found at a fabric store. To keep your scissors sharp and in good working order, be sure to use these scissors on fabric only. **Pinking shears** cut a decorative edge that will help prevent fraying. A **rotary cutter and mat** are helpful but not necessary.

You will probably need a **seam ripper** to safely rip out adjustments and mistakes.

I recommend that you have a 6″ × 12″ rectangular **ruler**, or even a 6″ × 24″. Having both would be an asset when making bags, as these rulers can be useful when cutting strips of fabric for the handles.

Use **chalk** or **wax marking pencils** to accurately transfer important construction lines and matching points from the patterns to the fabric.

Any **pins** that are sold at sewing or fabric shops will work fine.

Making and Using the Patterns

The patterns in this book are found on the pullout sheets and are usually presented either as half-pattern pieces, which need to be cut on the fold of the fabric, or as corner templates, which are traced onto precut fabric rectangles. The rectangles are then trimmed along the traced lines.

The easiest way to create the patterns or corner templates for your chosen bag is to lay a piece of white paper over the pattern on the pullout sheet and trace it. Taping the pullout sheet to a window, with the paper on top, will help the lines show through. If the pattern is larger than your paper, simply tape sheets of paper together to create a piece large enough to trace the pattern.

Using the Half-Patterns

You have two options for using the half-patterns to cut
out the fabric pieces.

Option 1:
Fold your fabric along the straight grain, and place the center fold
line of the pattern on the fold. You may want to pin the layers
together to keep them from shifting. Trace around the pattern
with a marking pencil, and cut out the piece through both layers.
If you have 2 pieces to cut from the same pattern, either fold 2
layers together, or fold 2 pieces of fabric separately and stack them,
matching the folds. Trace around the pattern, and cut out the pieces
through all the layers at the same time.

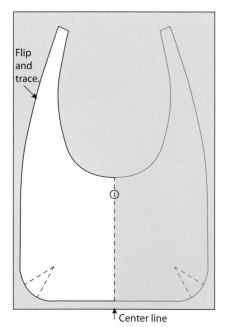

*Place pattern on fold. Trace around
pattern, and cut through all layers.*

Option 2:
Place the pattern onto a single layer of fabric with the center fold line
on the straight grain. Trace around all sides except the center fold
line. Flip the pattern over, keeping the center fold line in place, and
trace the other half of the design. If you have 2 or more pieces to cut
from the same pattern, simply place the layers right sides together.
Trace around the pattern, and cut out the pieces through all the
layers at the same time.

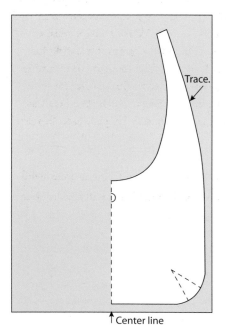

Place pattern on center fold line, and trace one side.

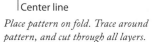

Flip pattern over, and trace other side.

Using the Corner Templates

Many of the rectangular pieces are cut according to cutting measurements given in the instructions, and then corner templates are used to round out the corners. Always cut the rectangles on the straight grain of the fabric, unless otherwise noted.

Trace the required corner template (as given in the project instructions) onto a piece of white paper. Cut around the curve, and square up the top and side. Position the corner on the corresponding fabric piece, aligning the side and bottom edges, and trace the curve. Trim along the traced line. Be sure to also mark the pieces according to the diagrams given in the project instructions. Flip the piece over, and repeat with the opposite corner or corners.

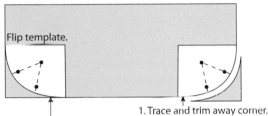

Flip template.

1. Trace and trim away corner.
2. Flip corner template over and repeat.

Use corner templates to shape rectangular pieces.

Using Iron-on Interfacing

The thickness of the fabric and the bag's design will determine the thickness or stiffness of the interfacing you should use. If I were to make a clutch out of quilting cotton, I would use medium or heavyweight interfacing to give the lighter-weight fabric more body. However, if I were to use home decorator fabric, I would use a lighter interfacing so it doesn't become too stiff. For bags whose form is crucial to the design (such as the Rebecca Bag, page 128), it is best to use heavy-weight interfacing; for bags whose design requires a looser, more natural shape, it is better to use lightweight rather than heavyweight interfacing.

The thicker and heavier the interfacing, the more challenging the project will be to sew. So it is best for beginners to start off with lightweight interfacing and then move up to heavier-weight interfacing with practice. Shape-Flex (from C&T Publishing) is a good all-purpose fusible interfacing.

Always test interfacing on a scrap to be sure you get the desired result. You are also testing for shrinkage and adhesive show-through. When you are satisfied that you have chosen the correct interfacing for your fabric, place the fabric piece on your ironing board *wrong side up*. Center the interfacing on top of it, *adhesive side down*. Follow the manufacturer's instructions precisely, because each fusible is different.

❊ caution ❊ If the interfacing is ironed with the fusible side up, the interfacing will stick to your iron rather than to the fabric.

Attaching Hook-and-Loop Tape

Most people use magnetic snaps when making the closure for a bag or a clutch. But for some bags, such as a pencil case or schoolbag, it is more practical to use hook-and-loop tape. Hook-and-loop tape is also used in places where magnets cannot be attached, such as on wallets, and can also be used for attaching pockets and other parts.

1. Cut a piece of sew-in hook-and-loop tape the size you need.

2. Separate the 2 parts, and place 1 piece of the hook-and-loop tape on the fabric. Sew around all 4 edges, backtacking at the starting and ending points.

3. Place the other piece of hook-and-loop tape on the corresponding piece of fabric, and sew around all 4 edges, backtacking at the starting and ending points.

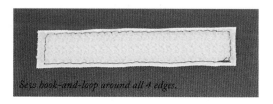

Sew hook-and-loop around all 4 edges.

Shortening Zipper Length

For the bags in this book requiring zippers, an all-purpose zipper is all that is needed.

If you want to use a zipper that is too long, you can shorten it to fit, as follows: Measure the desired length of the zipper to find where the new bottom stop should be. Machine zigzag over the coil or stitch over the coil several times by hand to create a new bottom stop. Trim away the excess zipper ½″ below the stitching.

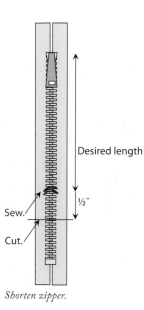

Desired length

½″

Sew.

Cut.

Shorten zipper.

Adding a Magnetic Snap

You should attach the magnetic snap following the manufacturer's instructions, but here's how it is generally done:

Position metal support over snap position.

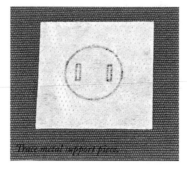
Trace metal support piece.

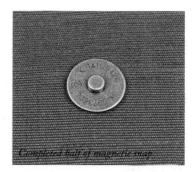
Snip holes for prongs through all layers.

1. Cut a piece of interfacing approximately 1½″ × 1½″. Center the interfacing over the marked snap position on the wrong side of the fabric and fuse it in position. Then center the metal support piece on top of the interfacing, over the marked snap position.

2. Trace around the metal support piece, including the holes for the prongs.

3. Carefully snip the holes for the prongs, through all the layers.

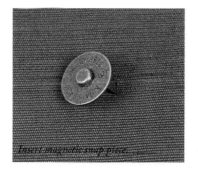
Insert magnetic snap piece.

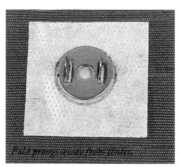
Fold prong away from center.

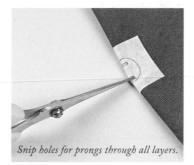
Completed half of magnetic snap.

4. From the right side of the fabric, insert the prongs of a magnetic snap piece.

5. Place the metal support of the snap over the prongs. Fold the prongs away from the center over the disc.

6. Repeat Steps 1–5 to attach the other half of the magnetic snap to the corresponding piece of fabric.

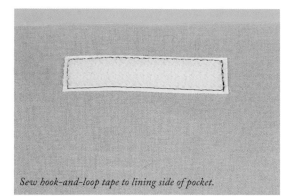

Sew hook-and-loop tape to lining side of pocket.

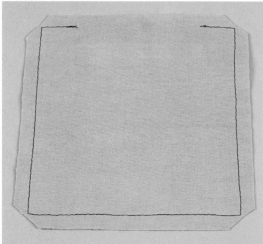

Sew pocket, leaving opening for turning.

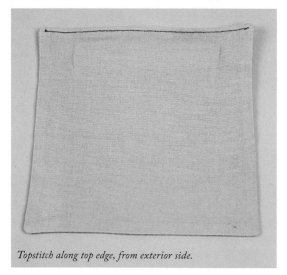

Topstitch along top edge, from exterior side.

Making a Pocket

There are several ways to make pockets. Here is my favorite method to achieve a strong pocket. It uses two layers of fabric and includes a hook-and-loop closure, but you can omit the closure if you don't want it.

1. Cut out the pocket pieces as described in the project instructions, or cut 2 pieces of pocket fabric approximately 7″ wide × 6″–7″ deep.

2. Cut a 4″–5″ length of hook-and-loop tape for the pocket closure, if you are adding one. Center one piece of the hook-and-loop tape on the right side of a pocket fabric piece, with the top edge of the tape 1″ from the top edge of the fabric, and sew around all 4 edges, backtacking at the starting and ending points. This will become the lining side of the pocket.

3. Pin the pocket pieces together with right sides facing, and sew around all 4 sides using a ½″ seam allowance, leaving 4″ unstitched along the top edge (nearest the hook-and-loop tape) for turning. Trim the corners.

4. Turn the pocket right side out, and use a sharp tool to carefully push the corners out. Fold the raw edges of the opening to the inside, and press the pocket. Pin the opening, and from the exterior side, topstitch the top edge ⅛″ from the edge, backtacking at both ends. The folded-in edges will be secured in the topstitching.

5. Position the pocket on the bag lining as described in the project instructions, with the hook-and-loop tape facing the lining. Fold back the pocket to reveal the hook-and-loop tape, and mark the corresponding location for the other piece of hook-and-loop tape onto the lining. The markings should be straight and centered on the lining.

Sew hook-and-loop tape to right side of bag lining.

6. Place the remaining piece of hook-and-loop tape over the markings on the bag lining, and sew around all 4 edges, backtacking at the starting and ending points.

7. Reposition the pocket on the bag lining, adhering the hook-and-loop tape pieces together. Topstitch the pocket in place—down one side, across the bottom, and up the other side, backtacking at both ends.

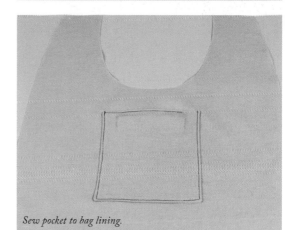

Sew pocket to bag lining.

Sewing Darts and Pleats

Darts

1. Transfer the A and B points from the pattern to the fabric. Fold the fabric, and match and pin the A points, with right sides together. Align and pin carefully, so the darts on the front and back pieces will match up perfectly when they're sewn together. Place another pin at point B.

2. Sew the dart seam from points A to B, back-tacking at both ends. Press the darts in the direction indicated in the project instructions

Pin, sew, and press darts.

Pleats

1. Referring to the pattern, fold each pleat on the fold line, in the direction indicated in the project instructions, and align the 2 match lines, with right sides together.

2. Pin the folded pleats to secure them. They will be stitched when the corresponding pieces are sewn together. However, you may also choose to baste them in place at this time.

Pin or baste pleats.

Making Bias Binding

Instructions are for making ½″-wide double-fold bias binding.

1. Cut bias strips 1⅞″ wide. Trim the ends of the strips at a 45° angle, if needed, before proceeding to Step 2.

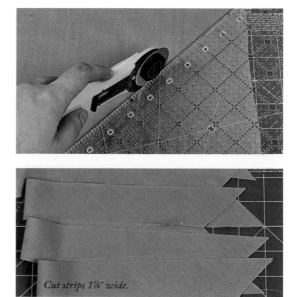

Cut strips 1⅞″ wide.

2. Place 2 strips right sides together, matching the 45° angles, and stitch along the 45° angle with a ¼″ seam allowance. Continue adding strips to achieve the length you need. Press all the seams open, and trim off the extra little triangles that extend past the edge of the strip.

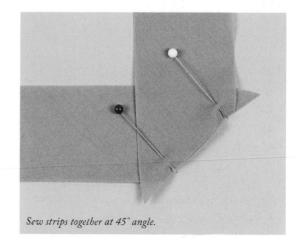

Sew strips together at 45° angle.

3. Fold the bias strip in half lengthwise, with the wrong sides together, and press to make a crease. Open the strip with the wrong side facing you. Fold in each side of the strip ⅜″, and press.

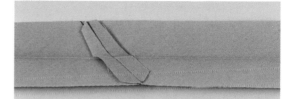

Fold strip in half lengthwise, and press.

4. Fold in half again along the first crease, and press.

Open out strip, fold in side edges, and press.

Fold again.

Place bias strip with cord in center.

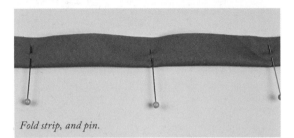

Fold strip, and pin.

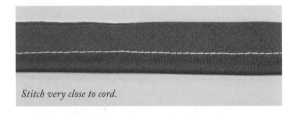

Stitch very close to cord.

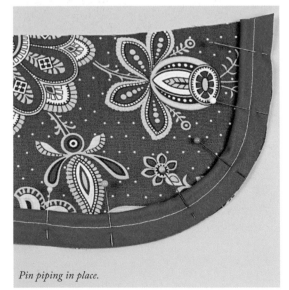

Pin piping in place.

Making Piping

Piping is a decorative trim or embellishment that you can buy, or you can easily make your own from bias strips and cording. To determine the width to cut the bias strips, measure the circumference of the cord and add 1″ for a seam allowance.

1. Cut bias strips, and piece them into the length you need (see Making Bias Binding, Steps 1 and 2, pages 16–17). Place the bias strip wrong side up with the cord in the center.

2. Fold the strip in half, align the raw edges, and pin.

3. Stitch very close to the cord using a zipper foot or a piping foot.

4. Lay the piping on the right side of the fabric, with the stitching directly over the seamline with a ½″ seam allowance. To apply piping to a curved seam, clip or notch the curved edge only as necessary to help the piping fit around the curve smoothly. Pin or baste in place.

Adding a Label

Adding a label to a completed bag makes the piece look more professional. Labels of cotton or linen are sold in stores. It is also a lot of fun to make or purchase personalized labels.

A label can be sewn to the bag lining or the bag exterior before construction, or it can be sewn to the bag exterior, through all the layers, after the bag is completed. Glue, fold, and press under the raw edges before sewing to prevent fraying.

A label can also be sewn into a seam on the bag exterior as it is being constructed. Fold the label in half, wrong sides together, and pin where desired before stitching the seam.

Glue raw edges of label, then press.

Levels of Difficulty

The projects have been rated with a ●, ●●, or ●●● level of difficulty.

● These are the easiest projects to make. They have the fewest pieces to sew together and require only straight or matching curved seams. They usually have just a few features, such as simple darts or a pocket in the lining, and they generally have magnetic snap or hook-and-loop tape closures.

●● These projects have a few more pieces to sew together, but still require only straight or matching curved seams. They have added features, such as pleats or darts and sometimes a zipper, a pocket in the lining, or a handle that is made separately and must be attached.

●●● These projects generally have the most pieces to sew together. Some seams involve sewing a straight edge to a curved edge or smoothly sewing inside corners. They have the most features: a combination of pleats or darts, zippers, binding, and separate handles to make and attach.

Sew folded label into seam during construction.

{ choosing your fabric }

Many beginners are overwhelmed when trying to choose fabric. Becoming comfortable with selecting fabric will make it much easier to enjoy sewing for years to come! Let's start by taking a deep breath and imagining that we are at the fabric store.

At the Fabric Store

Regardless of how much fabric is available in the store, almost every fabric store organizes its fabric the same way. Once you understand how the store organizes fabric, you won't be overwhelmed, no matter how much fabric is displayed.

Fabric is usually organized by the type of material and then grouped by color. Quilting-weight cotton is usually the largest section. Home decorator and quilting-weight cotton are the only types of fabric you will need for the projects presented in this book.

Consider the Bag Shape and Size

When choosing a fabric, you should always have in mind the pattern you are going to make. A fabric may be pretty, but it might not look good in that particular pattern. Initially, you will find it much easier if you consider fabrics that are similar to the pictures in this book; later, when you are more experienced, it will be easier to look at other styles of prints.

The choice of print also depends on the size of the bag you're going to make. The basic principle—for beginners, anyway—is that the smaller the size of the bag, the smaller the fabric's print should be.

Pick the Main Color First

If you are planning to sew a quilt, you have to choose many colors. However, for a bag you'll need a maximum of two or three different colors. First, choose the color you like best for the main color. If you have trouble selecting a second color, remember that the shop staff is always willing to help. Be sure to choose the main color yourself, or your bag will end up looking like someone else's project. Part of the satisfaction you will gain from your creation is knowing that you, and not someone else, chose the fabric.

Two Tips for Choosing Fabrics

Choose the main fabric, and then for a second color, select a contrasting color with the same style. It is a good idea to choose the second color from a fabric line designed by the designer of the main fabric. The designer has likely already chosen colors that work together well.

Online Ordering

If you must purchase fabric online, expect the unexpected to arrive. Why? The colors shown on your computer screen will be different in real life because of the limitations of computer screens and the quality of the images. Another thing that might surprise you about the fabric when it arrives is that the feel of the material; it can be very different from what you may have imagined.

It may be impossible to avoid purchasing online if your local quilt store does not have the selection you want, but there is a way to increase your success rate when ordering online. Let's say you would like to purchase a fabric from designer A. If your local fabric store doesn't carry that particular fabric, the store might have at least one or two fabrics from that line. After taking a look at and feeling the fabric, you will be able to guess what the fabric ordered online will be like.

Another way to lessen the failure rate is to purchase a charm pack (a package of several small squares of fabric) that includes the fabric you want. I love buying charm packs because they usually include the whole line in a small-size sample. If you get a charm pack, you will be able to look at all the colors in the line, and as a bonus create a patchwork fabric to use to make a bag.

Strive to Be a Satisfactionist, Not a Perfectionist

When selecting fabric, guard yourself against becoming a perfectionist, because if you do become one, your fabric shopping will never end. To be a perfectionist when shopping for fabric, you'll need to look at every fabric—but there are too many fabrics for this to be possible. Telling yourself that you can choose a fabric only after looking at all fabrics is the same as telling yourself that you can't choose any fabric.

If you are, say, around 70–80 percent satisfied when picking the fabric, then go for it.

Try not to think too much about it, and don't be afraid to have a trial-and-error mind-set! In the time that you spent trying to make a decision, you could have made another bag.

Small Bags

{ sunglasses case }

How can you keep your sunglasses safe? Invest an hour and make a sunglasses case! Add piping on the flap for a special touch. You can use either home decorator or quilting-weight cotton fabric.

Use the Sunglasses Case Front/Back and the Sunglasses Case Flap Corner patterns on pullout page P-2.

FINISHED SIZE: 7½″ × 3¾″

SKILL LEVEL:

WHAT YOU NEED

Fabric amounts are based on 44″-wide fabric.

¼ yard for exterior

¼ yard for lining

⅜ yard of 22″-wide fusible fleece interfacing

14mm magnetic snap

¾″ button

12¾″ of piping (optional): purchase or make your own (see Making Piping, page 18)

CUTTING THE PIECES

Follow the instructions in Making and Using the Patterns (page 9). Transfer all points and references to the fabric.

exterior

Cut 2 Front/Back pieces.

Cut 1 piece 7½″ × 4″ for the flap. Refer to the Flap diagram to mark the pieces and to trace and trim the bottom corners using the Sunglasses Case Flap Corner template.

lining

Cut 2 Front/Back pieces.

Cut 1 piece 7½″ × 4″ for the flap. Refer to the Flap diagram to mark the pieces and to trace and trim the bottom corners using the Sunglasses Case Flap Corner template.

interfacing

Cut 2 Front/Back pieces.

Cut 1 piece 7½″ × 4″ for the flap. Refer to the Flap diagram to mark the pieces and to trace and trim the bottom corners using the Sunglasses Case Flap Corner template.

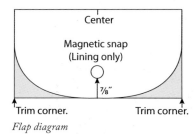

Flap diagram

Sewing the Exterior and Lining

1. Fuse the interfacing to the wrong side of the exterior pieces.

2. Attach the magnetic snap to the exterior front and on lining flap pieces as marked (see Adding a Magnetic Snap, page 13).

3. Sew the darts on the exterior front and back pieces, and the lining front and back pieces (see Sewing Darts and Pleats, page 16).

4. Press the darts on the front pieces toward the center. Press the darts on the back pieces toward the outside edge.

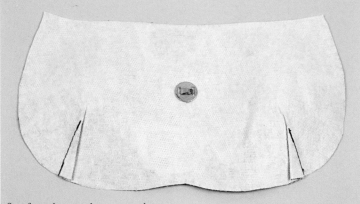

Sew front darts, and press toward center.

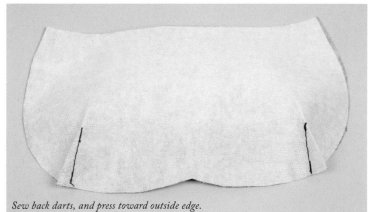

Sew back darts, and press toward outside edge.

5. Pin the front and back exterior pieces with the right sides together. The darts on the front and back pieces will be pressed in opposite directions, so they will lie flat.

6. Sew around the side and bottom edges, backtacking at each end. Notch the seam.

7. Repeat Steps 5 and 6 for the lining.

8. Press the exterior and lining seams open. Turn the exterior right side out. Insert the exterior inside the lining, with right sides together.

9. Pin the exterior and lining together around the top opening.

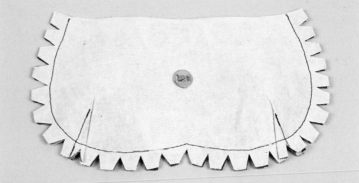

Sew side and bottom edges.

Insert exterior inside lining.

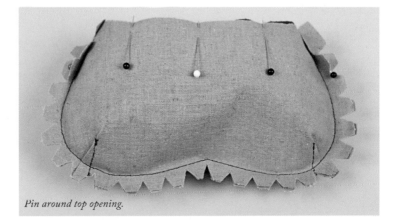

Pin around top opening.

10. Sew around the opening, leaving 3˝ unstitched for turning. Trim the corners at the tops of the seams. Turn right side out. Tuck the lining into the exterior. Press the opening, including the seam allowances of the unstitched opening, and pin.

11. Topstitch around the opening ⅛˝ from the edge. The folded-in edges will be secured in the topstitching.

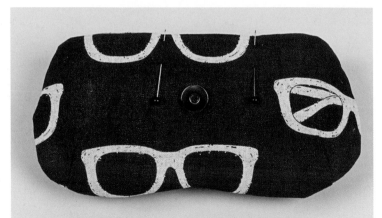

Turn, press, and pin opening.

Making the Flap

1. If you are adding the optional piping, baste it to the exterior flap around the curved edge (see Making Piping, page 18). Pin the exterior flap and lining flap with right sides together. Stitch around the flap, leaving 3˝ unstitched on the top straight edge for turning. Trim the corners, and notch the curved seam. Trim the seam allowance to ¼˝.

2. Turn right side out. Press, and topstitch ⅛˝ from the curved seam only. Tuck in the seam allowances on the unstitched opening, press, and slipstitch the opening closed.

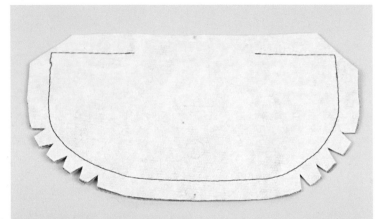

Stitch around flap, leaving 3˝ unstitched.

Topstitch curved seam only.

Finishing the Bag

1. Center the flap on the back of the exterior, with the straight edge along the flap stitching line, and pin in place. Check the position of the magnetic snap, and adjust the flap if needed.

2. Topstitch the flap in place, ⅛″ from the straight edge, backtacking at both ends.

3. Sew the button to the exterior flap in the desired location.

Finished! Enjoy the SUN!

Pin flap to back.

{sunglasses case}

{ pencil case }

This easy pencil case is a great project for using up fabrics left over from other projects. Use hook-and-loop tape if you plan to use it as a pencil case, or magnetic snaps work well if you're planning to use it for some other purpose. You can use either home decorator or quilting-weight cotton fabric. This makes a great back-to-school gift!

Use the Pencil Case Front/Back Corner and the Pencil Case Flap Corner patterns on pullout page P-4.

FINISHED SIZE: 7½″ × 3″

SKILL LEVEL: ●

WHAT YOU NEED

Fabric amounts are based on 44″-wide fabric.

1-fabric option

  ¼ yard for exterior

2-fabric option

  8½″ × 8″ for exterior front and back

  8⅛″ × 3¼″ for exterior flap

both options

In addition to the above, you will also need:

  ¼ yard for lining

  ⅜ yard of 22″-wide heavyweight fusible interfacing

  4″ of ½″-wide hook-and-loop tape

CUTTING THE PIECES

Follow the instructions in Making and Using the Patterns (page 9). Transfer all points and references to the fabric.

exterior

Cut 2 pieces 8½˝ × 4˝ for the front and back. Refer to the Front/Back diagram to mark the pieces and to trace and trim the bottom corners using the Pencil Case Front/Back Corner template.

Cut 1 piece 8⅛˝ × 3¼˝ for the flap. Refer to the Flap diagram to mark the pieces and to trace and trim the bottom corners using the Pencil Case Flap Corner template.

lining

Cut 2 pieces 8½˝ × 4˝ for the front and back. Refer to the Front/Back diagram to mark the pieces and to trace and trim the bottom corners using the Pencil Case Front/Back Corner template.

Cut 1 piece 8⅛˝ × 3¼˝ for the flap. Refer to the Flap diagram to mark the pieces and to trace and trim the bottom corners using the Pencil Case Flap Corner template.

interfacing

Cut 2 pieces 8½˝ × 4˝ for the front and back. Refer to the Front/Back diagram to mark the pieces and to trace and trim the bottom corners using the Pencil Case Front/Back Corner template.

Cut 1 piece 8⅛˝ × 3¼˝ for the flap. Refer to the Flap diagram to mark the pieces and to trace and trim the bottom corners using the Pencil Case Flap Corner template.

tips ------------------

❋ *Do not use hook-and-loop tape from the stationery section of the store. It is often too thick and can damage your sewing machine needle. Use hook-and-loop tape intended for fabric; it is softer and easier to sew.*

❋ *When storing your hook-and-loop tape, be sure not to wrinkle it. Folds are okay, but wrinkles can create a challenge when you attach the tape to your project. If yours gets wrinkled, place a heavy object on top of it to help flatten it.*

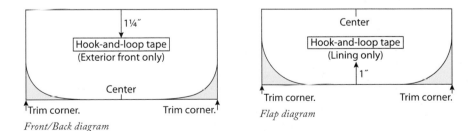

Front/Back diagram

Flap diagram

Sew hook-and-loop tape.

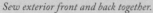

Sew exterior front and back together.

Sew lining front and back together, leaving 3˝ unstitched.

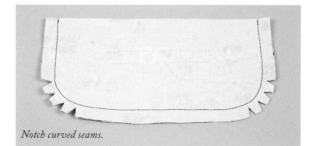

Notch curved seams.

Sewing the Exterior and Lining

1. Fuse the interfacing to the wrong side of the exterior pieces.

2. Separate the hook-and-loop tape, and attach the softer piece to the exterior front as marked (see Attaching Hook-and-Loop Tape, page 12). Sew the rougher half to the lining flap as marked.

3. Pin the exterior front and back pieces with the right sides together. Sew around the side and bottom edge, backtacking at both ends. Repeat with the lining front and back pieces, leaving 3˝ unstitched along the bottom edge for turning.

4. Notch the curved seams.

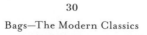

Making the Flap

1. Pin the exterior flap to the lining flap with the right sides together. Stitch only the curved seam, leaving the straight edge unstitched. Notch the curved seam, and trim the seam allowance to ¼˝.

2. Turn the flap right side out. Press, and topstitch ⅛˝ from the seam.

Assembling the Exterior and Lining

1. Press the exterior and lining seams open. Turn the exterior right side out.

2. Center the flap on the back piece of the case, with the exterior sides together, aligning the raw edges. Pin and baste in place.

3. Insert the exterior inside the lining, with right sides together, sandwiching the flap between the exterior and the lining.

4. Pin the exterior and lining together around the opening of the case.

5. Sew around the opening. Trim the corners at the tops of the seams. Turn right side out. Slipstitch the opening in the lining closed. Tuck the lining into the exterior. Press the top opening of the case.

6. Topstitch around the opening ⅛˝ from the edge.

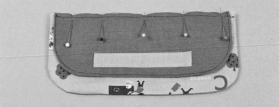

Press and topstitch flap.

Pin and baste flap to exterior back.

Insert exterior inside lining.

Pin around opening.

Turn, and press.

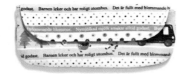

{ betty wallet }

The exterior of this wallet can be made using one piece of fabric (1-fabric option) or using many pieces sewn together and treated as one (patchwork option). Once you learn how to make bias binding, you'll love the effect it adds—and it's easier than it looks! If necessary, consider adding interfacing on both the exterior and lining pieces to give extra body and stability to the wallet. You can use either home decorator or quilting-weight cotton fabric.

Use the Betty Wallet Exterior/Lining/Pocket Corner and the Betty Wallet Card Holder patterns on pullout page P-1.

FINISHED SIZE: 4˝ × 8˝ (closed)

SKILL LEVEL: ●●

WHAT YOU NEED

Fabric amounts are based on 44˝-wide fabric.

¼ yard for 1-fabric option exterior or 4–5 different fabrics, approximately 6˝ × 9˝ each, for patchwork option exterior

¼ yard for lining

¼ yard for pocket and card holder

⅜ yard for binding (to make your own bias binding, see page 16) OR

1 yard of ½˝-wide double-fold bias binding (purchased)

¼ yard of 22˝-wide heavyweight fusible interfacing

3˝ of ⅛˝-wide elastic

1˝ button

CUTTING THE PIECES

Follow the instructions in Making and Using the Patterns (page 9). Transfer all points and references to the fabric.

exterior

1-fabric option

Cut 1 square 8″ × 8″ for the exterior. Refer to the Exterior/Lining diagram (page 34) to mark the pieces and to trace and trim all 4 corners using the Betty Wallet Exterior/Lining/Pocket Corner template.

patchwork option

A ¼″ seam allowance is included.

Cut piece A: 5¼″ × 8″.

Cut piece B: 1″ × 8″.

Cut piece C: 2¾″ × 4¼″.

Cut piece D: 2¾″ × 4¼″.

Make the exterior patchwork from pieces A, B, C, and D following the Patchwork exterior illustration, using ¼″ seams. Press the seams, and topstitch the patched exterior as shown. Trim, if needed, to 8″ × 8″. Then refer to the Exterior/Lining diagram (page 34) to mark the pieces and to trace and trim all 4 corners using the Betty Wallet Exterior/Lining/Pocket Corner template.

Trim patchwork exterior. Note: The wallet in this photo has 5 fabrics instead of 4. You can create your own patchwork however you like it best.

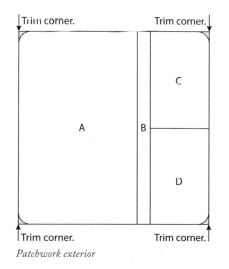

Patchwork exterior

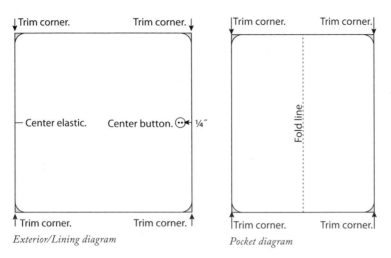

Trim corner.   Trim corner.

— Center elastic.   Center button. ⊙← ¼″

Trim corner.   Trim corner.

Exterior/Lining diagram

Trim corner.   Trim corner.

Fold line

Trim corner.   Trim corner.

Pocket diagram

Baste elastic loop in place.

lining

Cut 1 square 8″ × 8″ for the lining. Refer to the Exterior/ Lining diagram to mark the pieces and to trace and trim all 4 corners using the Betty Wallet Exterior/Lining/ Pocket Corner template.

pocket and card holder

Cut 1 piece 6½″ × 8″ for the pocket. Refer to the Pocket diagram to mark the pieces and to trace and trim all 4 corners using the Betty Wallet Exterior/Lining/ Pocket Corner template.

Cut 1 Card Holder piece, taking extra care to transfer the fold lines and place- ment lines accurately.

interfacing

Cut 1 square 8″ × 8″. Refer to the Exterior/Lining dia- gram to mark the pieces and to trace and trim all 4 corners using the Betty Wallet Exterior/Lining/ Pocket Corner template.

Sewing the Exterior

1. Fuse the interfacing to the wrong side of the exterior piece.

2. Fold the elastic in half to make a loop. Center the elastic loop on the side edge of the exterior as marked; baste the elastic loop in place.

Making the Pocket and Card Holder

pocket

1. Fold the pocket in half lengthwise along the marked fold line, wrong sides together, and press.

2. Topstitch ⅛″ from the fold.

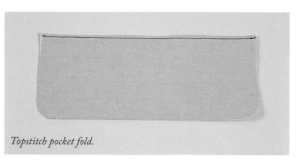

Topstitch pocket fold.

card holder

1. Referring to the markings on the pattern, fold the card holder, wrong sides together, along Fold Line 1, and press. From the right side, bring Fold Line 1 to Placement Line 1. Press.

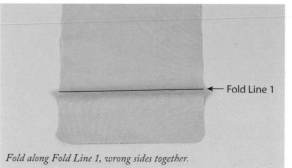

← Fold Line 1

Fold along Fold Line 1, wrong sides together.

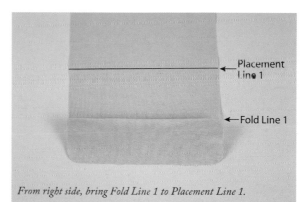

← Placement Line 1

←Fold Line 1

From right side, bring Fold Line 1 to Placement Line 1.

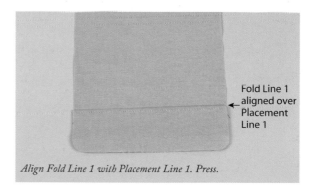

Fold Line 1 aligned over Placement Line 1

Align Fold Line 1 with Placement Line 1. Press.

Fold Fold Line 4 to wrong side, and press.

Topstitch 4 folds.

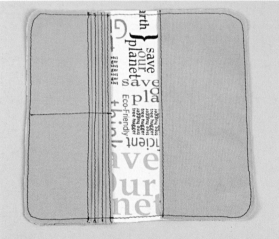

Sew card holder and pocket to lining.

2. Repeat with Fold Lines and Placement Lines 2 and 3.

3. Fold Line 4 should be folded toward the wrong side of the card holder. Press.

4. Topstitch each of the 4 folds ⅛″ from the edge.

5. Place the pocket and the card holder onto the lining as shown, aligning the corners and raw edges, and baste. Stitch a line down the center of the card holder to make 2 card-size pockets, back-tacking at both ends.

Adding Bias Binding

1. Refer to Making Bias Binding, page 16, to make 1 yard of ½"-wide double-fold bias binding, or use purchased binding.

2. Place the exterior and the lining with wrong sides together, making sure the elastic loop on the exterior is placed over either the pocket or the card holder. Baste around the edges. Unfold the bias binding, and press a short edge under ¼". Working from the exterior side and starting along a straight edge, begin pinning the raw edge of the binding to the outside edge of the wallet, with right sides together.

3. Pin the binding in place all the way around, easing around the curves so they fit smoothly. When you reach the end, lap the binding over the folded-in end. Trim away the excess binding, leaving a ½" overlap. Complete the pinning.

4. Stitch the binding in place along the crease line closest to the edge. Fold the binding over toward the lining to encase the raw edges. Pin in place through all the layers.

5. Topstitch the binding ⅛" from the inner fold of the binding, through all the layers. Sew the button to the exterior as marked.

Press short end of binding under ¼", and begin pinning.

Pin binding to wallet, easing corners and preparing to overlap short ends.

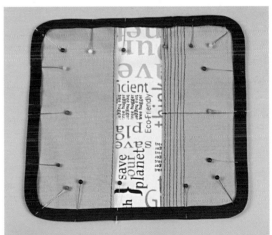

Pin binding in place through all layers.

{wristlet zipper purse}

Make this purse with or without the wrist strap. Learn to add a zipper while making this project. Make the top and pleat panels using different or the same fabric. You can use heavyweight home decorator or quilting-weight cotton.

Use the Wristlet Zipper Purse Top Panel Corner (large or small), the Wristlet Zipper Purse Pleat Panel Corner (used for both sizes), the Wristlet Zipper Purse Pleat Panel (large or small), the Wristlet Zipper Purse Exterior Back and Lining Front/Back Corner (large or small), and the three Wristlet Zipper Purse Corsage Petals (optional) patterns on pullout page P-2.

FINISHED SIZE: 9½″ × 5¼″ (large) or 6″ × 4¾″ (small)

SKILL LEVEL: ●●○

WHAT YOU NEED

Fabric amounts are based on 44″-wide fabric.

large or small

1-fabric option

> ¼ yard for top panel, pleat panel, and exterior back

2-fabric option

> ⅛ yard for top panel
>
> ¼ yard for pleat panel and exterior back

both options

> *In addition to the above, you will also need:*
>
> ⅛ yard for wristlet strap (optional)
>
> ¼ yard for lining
>
> ¼ yard of 22″-wide lightweight fusible interfacing
>
> 10″ all-purpose zipper for large size
>
> 6″ all-purpose zipper for small size

optional corsage

> 3 fabric scraps, 3″ × 3″ each
>
> ½″ button

CUTTING THE PIECES

Follow the instructions in Making and Using the Patterns (page 9). Transfer all points and references to the fabric. Refer to the diagrams (page 40).

large

exterior

Cut 1 piece 10½″ × 3″ for the top panel. Refer to the Top Panel diagram to mark the pieces and to trace and trim the bottom corners using the Wristlet Zipper Purse Top Panel Corner: Large template.

Cut 1 piece 16½″ × 4¼″ for the pleat panel. Refer to the Pleat Panel: Large diagram to trace and trim the bottom corners using the Wristlet Zipper Purse Pleat Panel Corner template. Using the Wristlet Zipper Purse Pleat Panel: Large template, align the template along the top edge of the fabric, and mark the top row of pleats. Move the template to the lower edge, and mark the bottom row of pleats.

Cut 1 piece 11⅛″ × 6¼″ for the back. Refer to the Exterior Back and Lining Front/Back diagram to mark the pieces and to trace and trim all 4 corners using the Wristlet Zipper Purse Exterior Back and Lining Front/Back Corner: Large template.

optional wristlet strap

Cut 1 strip 3″ × 17″ for the strap.

lining

Cut 2 pieces 11⅛″ × 6¼″ for the front and back. Refer to the Exterior Back and Lining Front/Back diagram to mark the pieces and to trace and trim all 4 corners using the Wristlet Zipper Purse Exterior Back and Lining Front/Back Corner: Large template.

interfacing

Cut 2 pieces 11⅛″ × 6¼″ for the front and back, and then trace and trim all 4 corners using the Wristlet Zipper Exterior Back and Lining Front/Back Corner: Large template.

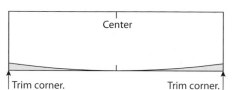

Top Panel diagram

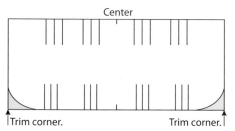

Pleat Panel: Large diagram

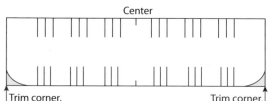

Pleat Panel: Small diagram

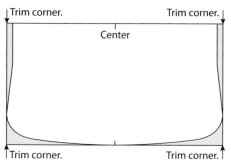

Exterior Back and Lining Front/Back diagram

Cut 1 piece 7″ × 2½″ for the top panel. Refer to the Top Panel diagram to mark the pieces and to trace and trim the bottom corners using the Wristlet Zipper Purse Top Panel Corner: Small template.

Cut 1 piece 10¼″ × 4¼″ for the pleat panel. Refer to the Pleat Panel: Small diagram to trace and trim the bottom corners using the Wristlet Zipper Purse Pleat Panel Corner template. Using the Wristlet Zipper Purse Pleat Panel: Small template, align the template along the top edge of the fabric, and mark the top row of pleats. Move the template to the lower edge, and mark the bottom row of pleats.

Cut 1 piece 7⅝″ × 5¾″ for the back. Refer to the Exterior Back and Lining Front/Back diagram to mark the pieces and to trace and trim all 4 corners using the Wristlet Zipper Purse Exterior Back and Lining Front/Back Corner: Small template.

optional wristlet strap

Cut 1 strip 1¾″ × 15″ for the strap.

lining

Cut 2 pieces 7⅝″ × 5¾″ for the front and back. Refer to the Exterior Back and Lining Front/Back diagram to mark the pieces and to trace and trim all 4 corners using the Wristlet Zipper Purse Exterior Back and Lining Front/Back Corner: Small template.

interfacing

Cut 2 pieces 7⅝″ × 5¾″ for the front and back, and then trace and trim all 4 corners using the Wristlet Zipper Purse Exterior Back and Lining Front/Back Corner: Small template.

optional corsage

Cut 1 of each petal using the Wristlet Zipper Purse Corsage Petals patterns.

Sewing the Pleat Panel and Top Panel

1. Pin the top row of pleats along the top edge of the pleat panel (see Sewing Darts and Pleats, page 16). Make sure the pleats fold toward the center.

2. Pin the pleated edge of the pleat panel to the curved edge of the top panel with right sides together. Stitch, backtacking at both ends. Press the seam allowance toward the top panel, and notch the curved seam. Topstitch the top panel ⅛″ from the seam.

Adding the Strap

1. Fold the strap in half lengthwise, with the wrong sides together, and press to make a crease. Open the strap with the wrong side facing you. For the large size, fold in each side of the strap ½″, and press. For the small size, fold in each side of the strap to the center crease, and press. For both, fold in half again along the first crease, and press. Topstitch ⅛″ away from the folded-in sides.

2. Fold the finished strap in half crosswise. Pin and baste it onto the left side edge of the top panel, with the center crease ¾″ down from the top edge.

Pin top row of pleats on pleat panel.

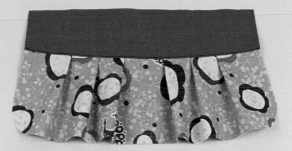

Sew pleat panel to top panel, and topstitch.

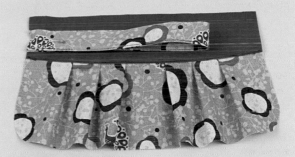

Pin strap to left side edge of top panel.

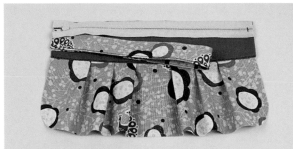

Position zipper on top panel, and trim tape if needed.

Pin lining front to top panel, with zipper in between.

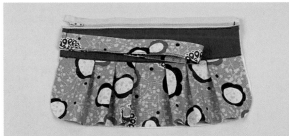

Topstitch top panel close to zipper coils.

Attach exterior back and lining to other side of zipper.

Installing the Zipper

1. Referring to the photo, close the zipper, and place it on the top panel with right sides together. Position the zipper pull ⅝″ from the side edge of the top panel, and then align the edge of the zipper tape along the upper raw edge of the top panel. Trim the excess zipper tape from the opposite side edge, but not closer than ¼″ from the zipper stop. If you need to trim away more of the zipper, see Shortening Zipper Length (page 12).

2. Pin the zipper to the top panel. Using a zipper foot, stitch the zipper to the top panel ⅛″ from the edge of the tape, leaving a ½″ seam allowance at both ends. Backtack at both ends.

3. Fuse the interfacing to the wrong side of the lining front. Pin together the top edges of the lining front and the top panel, with right sides facing. The zipper will now be between the top panel and the lining.

4. Using a zipper foot, sew the 3 layers together close to the zipper coils, leaving a ½″ seam allowance at both ends. Backtack at both ends.

5. Flip the lining over to the wrong side, and press. Topstitch the top panel close to the zipper coils through all the layers, leaving a ½˝ seam allowance at both ends.

6. Repeat Steps 2–5 to attach the exterior back and lining back pieces to the other side of the zipper.

Assembling the Exterior and Lining

1. Open the zipper before continuing. Pin the bottom row of pleats along the lower edge of the pleat panel. Place the exterior front and back pieces with right sides together, flipping the zipper coil toward the lining. Pin and stitch down one side, across the bottom, and up the opposite side (but not over the zipper coil), backtacking at both ends. *When stitching the exterior, do not sew into the lining.*

2. Pin the lining front and back pieces with right sides together, and sew in the same manner as in Step 1, but now sew carefully over the zipper coil. Leave 4˝ unstitched along the bottom edge for turning. Notch the curved seams. Trim the exterior and lining to a ¼˝ seam allowance.

3. Turn the purse right side out through the opening in the lining. Using a turning tool, push out the curved corners. Press the purse flat. Slipstitch the opening closed.

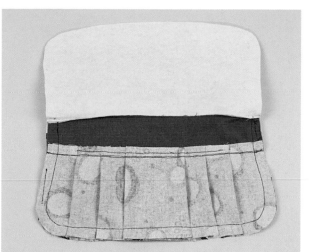

Sew exterior front and back together.

Sew lining front and back together.

{wristlet zipper purse}

Making the Corsage

1. Layer the 3 petals, right side up and with the largest on the bottom. Draw a ⅝″ circle in the center of the top layer, as indicated on the pattern.

2. Stitch a running stitch around the drawn circle through all the layers, pull the thread to gather, and fasten to secure. Place the button in the center of the gathered circle. Sew the button in place through all the layers. Position the corsage on the purse at the desired location. Sew in place.

Stitch running stitch around circle.

Sew button in place.

{wristlet zipper purse}

Clutches

{ glenda clutch }

This is a great project for beginners or anyone wanting a quick, beautiful gift. Also, if you would like to use up some leftover fabric, it is the perfect project to get started on! Choose the perfect button to make it uniquely your own. You can use either home decorator or quilting-weight cotton fabric.

Use the Glenda Clutch Front/Back Corner and the Glenda Clutch Flap Corner patterns on pullout page P-3.

FINISHED SIZE:
approximately 7¾″ × 5″ × 1″

SKILL LEVEL: ●●

WHAT YOU NEED

Fabric amounts are based on 44″-wide fabric.

¼ yard for exterior

¼ yard for lining

½ yard of 22″-wide medium-weight fusible interfacing

18mm magnetic snap

1″–2″ button or bead (optional)

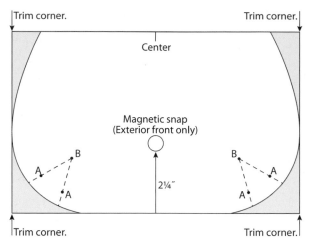

Front/Back diagram

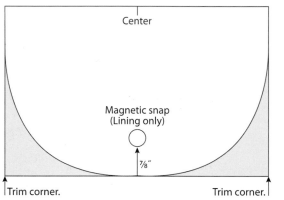

Flap diagram

CUTTING THE PIECES

Follow the instructions in Making and Using the Patterns (page 9). Transfer all points and references to the fabric.

exterior

Cut 2 pieces 10⅜″ × 6½″ for the front and back. Refer to the Front/Back diagram to mark the pieces and to trace and trim all 4 corners using the Glenda Clutch Front/Back Corner pattern.

Cut 1 piece 8¾″ × 5½″ for the flap. Refer to the Flap diagram to mark the pieces and to trace and trim the bottom corners using the Glenda Clutch Flap Corner pattern.

lining

Cut 2 pieces 10⅜″ × 6½″ for the front and back. Refer to the Front/Back diagram to mark the pieces and to trace and trim all 4 corners using the Glenda Clutch Front/Back Corner pattern.

Cut 1 piece 8¾″ × 5½″ for the flap. Refer to the Flap diagram to mark the pieces and to trace and trim the bottom corners using the Glenda Clutch Flap Corner pattern.

interfacing

Cut 2 pieces 10⅜″ × 6½″ for the front and back. Refer to the Front/Back diagram to mark the pieces and to trace and trim all 4 corners using the Glenda Clutch Front/Back Corner pattern.

Cut 1 piece 8¾″ × 5½″ for the flap. Refer to the Flap diagram to mark the pieces and to trace and trim the bottom corners using the Glenda Clutch Flap Corner pattern.

Sewing the Exterior and Lining

1. Fuse the interfacing to the wrong side of the exterior pieces.

2. Attach the magnetic snap to the exterior front and lining flap pieces as marked (see Adding a Magnetic Snap, page 13).

3. Sew the darts on the exterior front and back pieces and on the lining front and back pieces (see Sewing Darts and Pleats, page 16).

4. Press the darts on the front pieces toward the center. Press the darts on the back pieces toward the outside edge.

5. Pin the front and back exterior pieces with the right sides together. The darts on the front and back pieces will be pressed in opposite directions, so they will lie flat. Sew around the side and bottom edges, backtacking at both ends. Notch the curved seam.

6. Repeat Step 5 with the lining front and back pieces, leaving 4″ unstitched along the bottom edge for turning.

Making the Flap

1. Pin the exterior flap to the lining flap with the right sides together. Stitch only the curved seam, leaving the straight edge unstitched. Notch the curved seam, and trim the seam allowance to ¼″.

2. Turn the flap right side out. Press, and topstitch ⅛″ from the seam.

Sew front darts, and press toward center.

Sew back darts, and press toward outside edge.

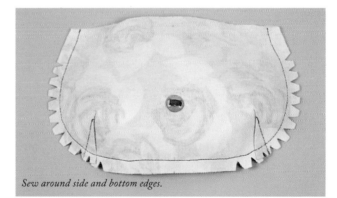

Sew around side and bottom edges.

Turn flap right side out, and topstitch.

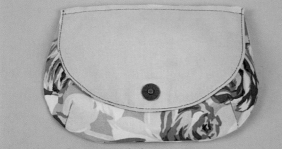

Pin and baste flap to exterior back.

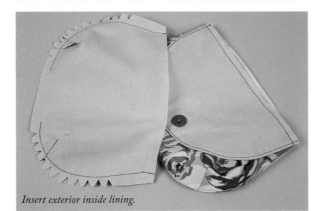

Insert exterior inside lining.

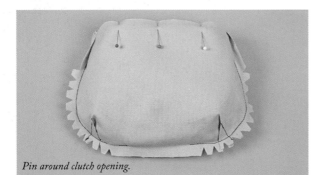

Pin around clutch opening.

Turn, press, and topstitch.

Assembling the Exterior and Lining

1. Press the exterior and lining seams open. Turn the exterior right side out.

2. Place the flap onto the back piece of the clutch, with the exterior sides together, aligning the raw edges. Pin and baste in place.

3. Insert the exterior inside the lining, with right sides together, sandwiching the flap between the exterior and the lining.

4. Pin the exterior and lining around the opening of the clutch.

5. Sew around the opening. Trim the corners at the tops of the seams. Turn right side out through the opening in the lining. Slipstitch the opening closed. Tuck the lining into the exterior. Press the top opening of the clutch.

6. Topstitch around the opening ⅛″ from the edge. Sew the button to the exterior flap in the desired location.

51

{ glenda clutch }

{ elegance pleated clutch }

Even a beginner can make this bag by following the instructions carefully! With the right fabrics and decoration, this bag can even go formal. Or, dress it down and it can be a makeup bag. You can use either home decorator or quilting-weight cotton fabric.

Use the Elegance Pleated Clutch Front/Back, the Elegance Pleated Clutch Side, the Elegance Pleated Clutch Flap Corner, and the Elegance Pleated Clutch Lining Front/Back patterns on pullout page P-3.

FINISHED SIZE:
approximately 10½″ × 6″

SKILL LEVEL: ●●

WHAT YOU NEED

Fabric amounts are based on 44″-wide fabric.

½ yard for exterior

⅜ yard for lining

⅝ yard of 22″-wide heavyweight fusible interfacing

18mm magnetic snap

1½″–1¾″ button or bead

CUTTING THE PIECES

Follow the instructions in Making and Using the Patterns (page 9). Transfer all points and references to the fabric.

exterior

Cut 2 Front/Back pieces.

Cut 4 Side pieces. (Trace the pattern and cut 2 pieces with right sides together. Flip the pattern over, and cut 2 more pieces).

Cut 1 piece 8⅜″ × 4½″ for the flap. Refer to the Flap diagram to mark the pieces and to trace and trim all 4 corners using the Elegance Pleated Clutch Flap Corner template.

lining

Cut 2 Lining Front/Back pieces.

Cut 1 piece 8⅜″ × 4½″ for the flap. Refer to the Flap diagram to mark the pieces and to trace and trim all 4 corners using the Elegance Pleated Clutch Flap Corner template.

interfacing

Cut 2 Lining Front/Back pieces.

Cut 1 piece 8⅜″ × 4½″ for the flap. Refer to the Flap diagram to mark the pieces and to trace and trim all 4 corners using the Elegance Pleated Clutch Flap Corner template.

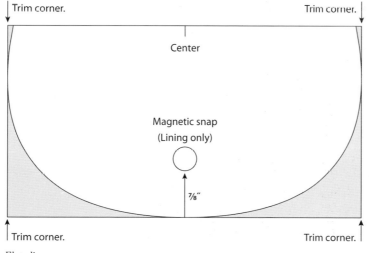

Flap diagram

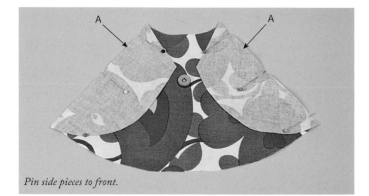

Pin side pieces to front.

Sew sides to front, press, and topstitch.

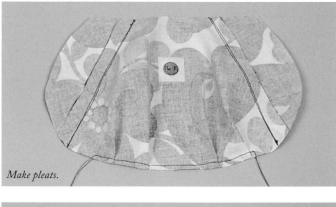

Make pleats.

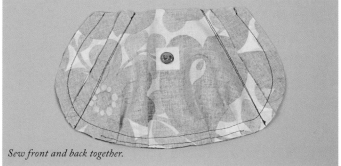

Sew front and back together.

Sewing the Exterior

1. Attach half of the magnetic snap (see Adding a Magnetic Snap, page 13) to the exterior front as marked (the other half is added later).

2. Pin a side piece to each side of the exterior front, matching the point A markings, with right sides together.

3. Stitch the seams, backtacking at both ends. Press the seams toward the sides. Topstitch the sides ⅛″ from the seams.

4. Make the pleats as indicated on the pattern (see Sewing Darts and Pleats, page 16). Make sure the pleats all fold toward the center.

5. Repeat Steps 2–4 for the back.

6. Pin the exterior front and back pieces with right sides facing. Sew around the side and bottom edges, backtacking at both ends. Notch the seam.

Sewing the Lining

1. Fuse the interfacing to the wrong side of the lining front, back, and flap pieces. Pin the lining front and back pieces with right sides together.

2. Sew around the side and bottom edges, backtacking at both ends and leaving 4″ unstitched along the bottom edge for turning. Notch the seam.

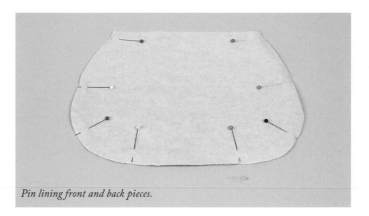

Pin lining front and back pieces.

Making the Flap

1. Attach the remaining magnetic snap piece onto the lining flap as marked.

2. Pin the exterior flap and lining flap with right sides together. Stitch only the curved seam, leaving the straight edge unstitched. Notch the curved seam, and trim the seam allowance to ¼″. Turn the flap right side out, and press.

3. Topstitch ⅛″ from the seam.

Turn flap right side out, press, and topstitch.

Pin and baste flap to exterior back.

Assembling the Exterior and Lining

1. Press the exterior and lining seams open. Turn the exterior right side out.

2. Position the flap onto the back piece of the clutch with exterior sides together and aligning the raw edges. Pin and baste in place.

3. Insert the exterior inside the lining, with right sides together, sandwiching the flap between the exterior and the lining.

4. Pin the exterior and lining together around the top opening of the clutch.

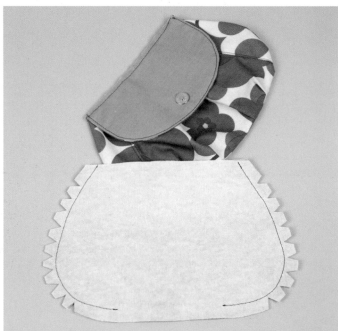
Insert exterior inside lining.

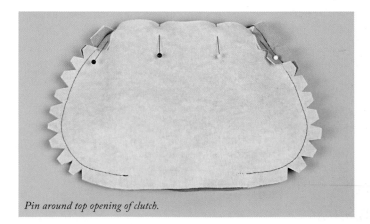
Pin around top opening of clutch.

5. Stitch around the opening. Trim the corners at the tops of the seams. Turn right side out through the opening left in the lining. Slipstitch the opening closed. Tuck the lining into the exterior. Press the top opening of the clutch.

6. Topstitch around the opening ⅛″ from the edge. Sew the button to the exterior flap in the desired location.

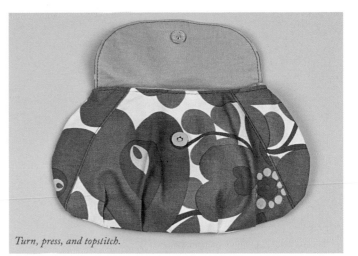

Turn, press, and topstitch.

{ elegance pleated clutch }

{ uptown clutch }

This clutch is perfect for a night out! You can use either home decorator or quilting-weight cotton fabric. Choose a print fabric for the sides and a matching solid-colored fabric for the center stripe. Make a clutch to match every outfit!

Use the Uptown Clutch Top Panel Corner, the Uptown Clutch Pleat Panel Corner, the Uptown Clutch Pleat Panel and the Uptown Clutch Flap Corner patterns on pullout page P–4. Use the Uptown Clutch Exterior Back and Lining Front/Back Corner pattern on pullout page P–1.

FINISHED SIZE: 15½″ × 7⅜″

SKILL LEVEL: ● ●

WHAT YOU NEED

Fabric amounts are based on 44″-wide fabric.

½ yard print for exterior

⅛ yard solid for exterior

½ yard for lining

1 yard of 22″-wide heavyweight fusible interfacing

18mm magnetic snap

CUTTING THE PIECES

Follow the instructions in Making and Using the Patterns (page 9). Transfer all points and references to the fabric.

exterior print

Cut 2 pieces 6⅞″ × 3⅝″ for the front top panels. Refer to the Front Top Panels diagram to trace and trim a corner from each piece using the Uptown Clutch Top Panel Corner template. Remember to flip the pattern over to trim the 2nd piece.

Cut 2 pieces 9⅝″ × 5¾″ for the pleat panels. Refer to the Pleat Panels diagram to trace and trim a corner from each piece using the Uptown Clutch Pleat Panel Corner template. Using the Uptown Clutch Pleat Panel template, align the template along the top edge of the fabric, and mark the top row of pleats. Move the template to the lower edge, and mark the bottom row of pleats. Remember to flip the patterns over to mark the 2nd piece.

Cut 1 piece 16½″ × 8⅜″ for the back. Refer to the Exterior Back and Lining Front/Back diagram (page 60) to mark the pieces and to trace and trim the corners using the Uptown Clutch Exterior Back and Lining Front/Back Corner template.

Cut 2 pieces 6½″ × 4½″ for the flap side panels. Refer to the Flap Side Panels diagram (page 60) to mark the pieces and to trace and trim the corners from each piece using the Uptown Clutch Flap Corner template. Remember to flip the pattern over to mark the 2nd piece.

exterior solid

Cut 1 piece 4″ × 8⅜″ for the front center panel.

Cut 1 piece 4″ × 4½″ for the flap center panel.

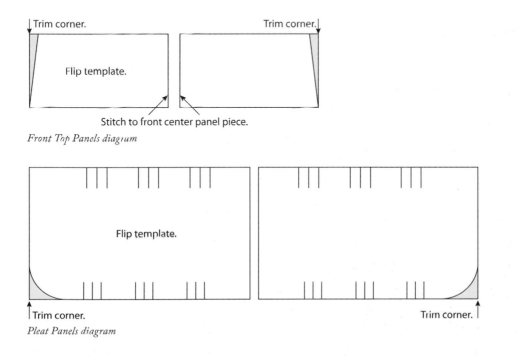

Trim corner.   Trim corner.

Flip template.

Stitch to front center panel piece.

Front Top Panels diagram

Flip template.

Trim corner.   Trim corner.

Pleat Panels diagram

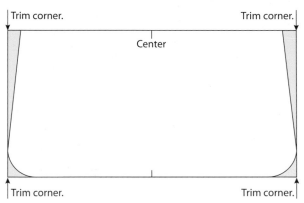

Exterior Back and Lining Front/Back diagram

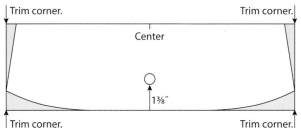

Flap Side Panels diagram

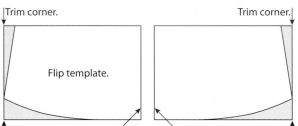

Lining Flap diagram

lining

Cut 2 pieces 16½″ × 8⅜″ for the lining front and back. Refer to the Exterior Back and Lining Front/Back diagram to mark the pieces and to trace and trim the corners using the Uptown Clutch Exterior Back and Lining Front/Back Corner template.

Cut 1 piece 15⅛″ × 4½″ for the lining flap. Refer to the Lining Flap diagram to mark the pieces and to trace and trim the corners using the Uptown Clutch Flap Corner template.

interfacing

Cut 2 pieces 16½″ × 8⅜″ for the exterior back and lining front and back. Refer to the Exterior Back and Lining Front/Back diagram to mark the pieces and to trace and trim the corners using the Uptown Clutch Exterior Back and Lining Front/Back Corner template.

Cut 1 piece 15⅛″ × 4½″ for the flap. Refer to the Lining Flap diagram to mark the pieces and to trace and trim the corners using the Uptown Clutch Flap Corner template.

Sewing the Exterior Panels

1. Make the top row of pleats along the straight edge of each pleat panel (see Sewing Darts and Pleats, page 16). Make sure the pleats on both sides fold toward the center.

2. Pin the pleated edges of the pleat panels to the bottom edges of the front top panels, right sides together. Stitch, backtacking at both ends. Press the seams toward the top panels.

3. Topstitch the top panels ⅛″ from the seams, and press.

4. Attach half of the magnetic snap (see Adding a Magnetic Snap, page 13) to the front center panel, centered with the top edge of the snap piece 2¼″ down from the top raw edge (the other half is added later).

5. Pin an assembled panel to the front center panel along the 8⅜″ sides, right sides together.

6. Stitch, backtacking at both ends. Press the seam allowance toward the front center panel. Sew the remaining assembled panel to the other side of the front center panel. Topstitch the front center panel ⅛″ from both seams to complete the front.

7. Pin the exterior back piece to the front, with right sides together, making the bottom row of pleats along the bottom edge of each pleat panel as marked.

8. Sew around the side and bottom edges, backtacking at both ends. Notch the rounded corner seam.

Make top row of pleats.

Sew pleat panels to top panels.

Pin assembled panel to front center panel.

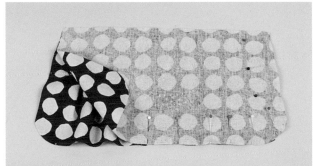

Pin front to back, and make bottom row of pleats.

{ uptown clutch }

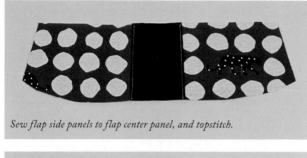

Sew flap side panels to flap center panel, and topstitch.

Sew flap to lining, turn, and press.

Making the Flap

1. Pin a flap side panel to the flap center panel along the 4½″ sides, right sides together. Stitch, backtacking at both ends. Press the seam toward the flap center panel.

2. Sew the remaining flap side panel to the other side of the flap center panel. Topstitch the flap center panel ⅛″ from both seams to complete the flap.

3. Fuse the interfacing to the wrong side of the lining flap. Attach the remaining magnetic snap piece to the lining flap as marked.

4. Pin the exterior flap to the lining flap with right sides facing. Stitch only the sides and curved bottom edge seam, leaving the top edge unstitched. Notch the curved seam, and trim the seam allowance to ¼″. Turn right side out, and press.

5. Topstitch the flap ⅛″ from the seam.

Sewing the Lining

1. Fuse the interfacing to the wrong side of the lining front and back. Pin the lining front and back pieces together with right sides facing.

2. Sew around the side and bottom edges, backtacking at each end and leaving 4″ unstitched along the bottom edge for turning. Notch the curved seam.

Assembling the Exterior and Lining

1. Press the exterior and lining seams open. Turn the exterior right side out.

2. Position the flap onto the back piece of the clutch, with exterior sides together, aligning the raw edges. Pin and baste in place.

3. Insert the exterior inside the lining, with right sides together, sandwiching the flap between the exterior and the lining.

4. Pin the exterior and lining together around the top opening of the clutch.

5. Sew around the opening. Trim the corners at the tops of the seams. Turn right side out through the opening left in the lining. Slipstitch the opening closed. Tuck the lining into the exterior. Press the top opening of the clutch.

6. Topstitch around the opening ⅛″ from the edge.

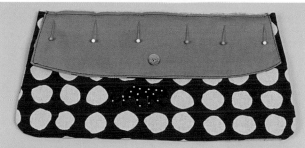

Pin and baste flap to exterior back.

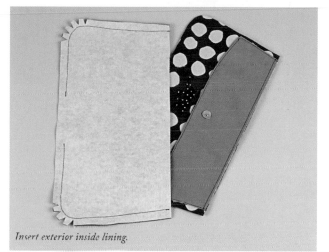

Insert exterior inside lining.

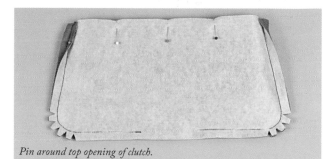

Pin around top opening of clutch.

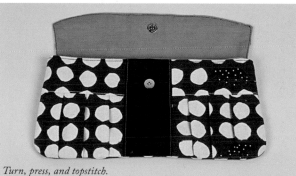

Turn, press, and topstitch.

Large Bags

{lovely clarissa bag}

The pleats give this lovely bag a round, pretty shape. Because it is very spacious, it is perfect to use as a diaper bag. You can use just one fabric or sew together pieces of different fabrics. This bag looks good with or without interfacing; however, without interfacing the bag will be softer and have less shape. The lining shows, so it is important to consider matching colors and patterns when choosing the fabrics for the exterior and lining.

Use the Lovely Clarissa Bag Front/Back and the Lovely Clarissa Bag Bottom patterns on pullout page P-1.

FINISHED SIZE:
approximately 19⅜″ × 14″ × 7¼″, plus 8¼″ handle

SKILL LEVEL: ●●

WHAT YOU NEED
Fabric amounts are based on 44″-wide fabric.

1⅛ yards or pieces sewn together to equal 1 yard for exterior

1⅛ yards for lining and pocket

1¾ yards of 22″-wide lightweight fusible interfacing

18mm magnetic snap

4″–5″ of hook-and-loop tape for pocket closure (optional; see Making a Pocket, page 14)

CUTTING THE PIECES

Follow the instructions in Making and Using the Patterns (page 9). Transfer all points and references to the fabric.

exterior

Cut 2 Front/Back pieces.

Cut 1 Bottom piece.

lining

Cut 2 Front/Back pieces.

Cut 1 Bottom piece.

Cut 2 pieces 8″ × 7″ for the pocket.

interfacing

Cut 2 Front/Back pieces.

Cut 1 Bottom piece.

Making the Pocket

Make the pocket (see Making a Pocket, page 14). Center the pocket on the right side of a lining front or back piece, with the lower (7″ finished) edge of the pocket placed 5″ from the bottom edge of the lining. Topstitch the pocket in place— down one side, across the bottom, and back up the other side, backtacking at both ends.

Sewing the Exterior and Lining

1. Fuse the interfacing to the wrong side of the exterior front, back, and bottom pieces.

2. Sew the darts on the exterior front and back pieces (see Sewing Darts and Pleats, page 16). Press the darts toward the center.

3. Pin the exterior front and back together with right sides facing. Stitch the side seams only down to the point C marking, as indicated on the pattern, backtacking at both ends. Press the side seams open.

4. Pin the assembled front and back to the bottom, with right sides facing and matching the side and center markings as indicated on the patterns. Pin at the 2 sides, the 2 centers, and then in between.

5. Sew around the bottom, backtacking at both ends. Notch the curved seam.

6. Attach the magnetic snap to the lining front and back pieces as indicated on the pattern (see Adding a Magnetic Snap, page 13).

7. Repeat Steps 2–5 with the lining pieces, pressing the darts toward the outside edge and leaving 4″ unstitched along the bottom seam for turning.

Sew darts, and press toward center.

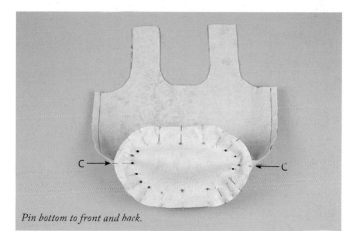

Pin bottom to front and back.

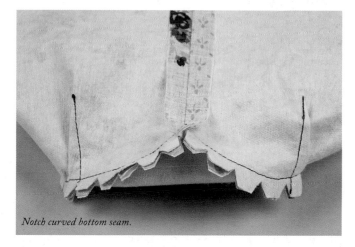

Notch curved bottom seam.

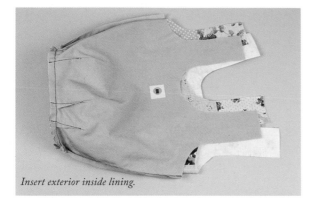

Insert exterior inside lining.

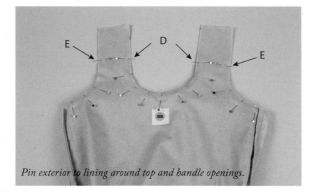

Pin exterior to lining around top and handle openings.

Assembling the Exterior and Lining

1. Turn the exterior right side out. Insert the exterior inside the lining, with right sides together.

2. Pin the exterior and the lining together around the front and back top openings and around the handle openings up to the point D and point E markings as indicated on the pattern.

3. Stitch the exterior to the lining from point D to point D on both the front and the back. Stitch the seams from point E to point E. Clip the curved seams.

4. Turn the bag right side out through the opening left in the lining. Slipstitch the opening closed. Tuck the lining into the exterior. Press the top opening of the bag.

Pin short edges of handles together.

Pin or baste turned-under edges of handles.

Finishing the Bag

1. Pin the short edges of the exterior handles together, and pin the short edges of the lining handles together, right sides facing.

2. Stitch the seams, backtacking at both ends. Press the seams open.

3. Turn under ½″ on the raw side edges of the exterior and lining handles, and press. Pin or baste the turned-under edges together.

4. Topstitch around the top and handle openings, ⅛″ from the edges. The turned-under edges will be secured in the topstitching.

{lovely clarissa bag}

{ chic hobo bag }

This very simple bag can be formal or informal, depending on your choice of fabric. There's only one pattern piece, so it's quick and easy to make. Since finding the perfect button, bead, or closure to match your fabric can be a challenge, consider choosing the button or bead first, and then picking the fabric. You can use either home decorator or quilting-weight cotton fabric.

Use the Chic Hobo Bag Front/Back pattern on pullout page P-2.

FINISHED SIZE:
approximately 15¾″ × 10½″, plus 12½″ handle

SKILL LEVEL: ◉

WHAT YOU NEED
Fabric amounts are based on 44″-wide fabric.

⅞ yard for exterior

1 yard for lining

1½ yards of 22″-wide medium-weight fusible interfacing

18mm magnetic snap

1½″–2⅜″ button or bead

4″–5″ of hook-and-loop tape for pocket closure (optional; see Making a Pocket, page 14)

CUTTING THE PIECES

Follow the instructions in Making and Using the Patterns (page 9). Transfer all points and references to the fabric.

exterior

Cut 2 Front/Back pieces.

lining

Cut 2 Front/Back pieces.

Cut 2 pieces 7″ × 6″ for the pocket.

interfacing

Cut 2 Front/Back pieces.

Making the Pocket

Make the pocket (see Making a Pocket, page 14). Center the pocket on the right side of a lining front or back piece, with the lower (6″ finished) edge of the pocket placed 3½″ from the bottom edge of the lining. Topstitch the pocket in place—down one side, across the bottom, and back up the other side, backtacking at both ends.

Sewing the Exterior and Lining

1. Fuse the interfacing to the wrong side of the exterior front and back pieces.

2. Sew the darts on the exterior front and back pieces (see Sewing Darts and Pleats, page 16). Press the darts on the front piece toward the center and on the back piece toward the outside seams.

3. Pin the exterior front and back pieces together around the outside edge, from the top of one handle to the top of the other, with right sides facing. The darts on the front and back pieces will be pressed in opposite directions, so they will lie flat.

4. Sew around the outside edge, backtacking at each end. Notch the curved seam. Press the seam open.

5. Attach the magnetic snap to the lining front and back pieces as indicated on the pattern (see Adding a Magnetic Snap, page 13).

6. Repeat Steps 2–4 with the lining pieces, leaving 5″ unstitched along the bottom edge for turning.

Sew and press darts.

Pin front and back together around outside edge.

Insert exterior inside lining.

C

Pin exterior and lining together between point C markings.

Assembling the Exterior and Lining

1. Turn the exterior right side out. Insert the exterior inside the lining, with right sides together.

2. Pin the exterior and the lining together around the inner curved seams on both the front and back between the point C markings, as indicated on the pattern.

3. Stitch the inner curved seams from point C to point C on both front and back. Clip the curved seams. Turn the bag right side out through the opening left in the lining. Slipstitch the opening closed.

Finishing the Bag

1. Pin the short edges of the exterior handle together, right sides facing.

2. Stitch the seam, backtacking at both ends. Press the seam open. Repeat for the lining handle.

3. Turn under ½″ on the raw side edges of the exterior and lining handle, and press. Pin or baste the turned-under edges together.

4. Topstitch around the inner curved seams, ⅛″ from the edges. The turned-under edges will be secured in the topstitching.

5. Sew the button or bead at the desired location.

Pin short edges of exterior handle together.

Stitch short edges of lining handle together.

Pin or baste turned-under edges of handle.

Topstitch around inner curved seams.

{veronica day bag}

The combination of the pleated front and round handle is what makes this bag so lovely. It is easy to make the pleats, but the curved handle is a bit of a challenge. You can use either home decorator or quilting-weight cotton fabric.

Use the Veronica Day Bag Exterior Front pattern on pullout page P-4. Use the Veronica Day Bag Lining Front/Back and Exterior Back, and the Veronica Day Bag Handle patterns on pullout page P-1.

FINISHED SIZE:
approximately 21¼″ × 13¾″, plus 8½″ handle

SKILL LEVEL: ● ● ●

WHAT YOU NEED

Fabric amounts are based on 44″-wide fabric.

1 yard for exterior front and back

¼ yard for exterior handles

¾ yard for lining front and back

¼ yard for lining handles

2 yards of 22″-wide heavyweight fusible interfacing

18mm magnetic snap

4″–5″ of hook-and-loop tape for pocket closure (optional; see Making a Pocket, page 14)

CUTTING THE PIECES

Follow the instructions in Making and Using the Patterns (page 9). Transfer all points and references to the fabric.

exterior

Cut 1 Exterior Front piece.

Cut 1 Exterior Back piece (the back does not have pleats).

exterior handles

Cut 2 Handle pieces.

lining

Cut 2 Lining Front/Back pieces.

Cut 2 pieces 7″ × 5″ for the pocket.

lining handles

Cut 2 Handle pieces.

interfacing

Cut 2 Lining Front/Back pieces.

Cut 2 Handle pieces.

Sewing the Exterior

1. Make the pleats on the exterior front (see Sewing Darts and Pleats, page 16). Make sure the pleats on both sides fold toward the center.

2. Pin a handle to the exterior front, with right sides facing and matching the center and point A markings as indicated on the patterns. Pin the centers, then at the point A markings, and then in between. Clip the exterior front piece between the point A markings only as necessary to help ease the fabric around the curve of the handle.

Make pleats on exterior front.

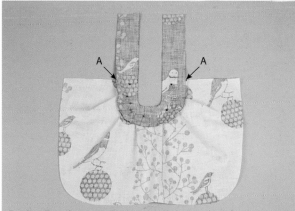

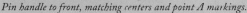

Pin handle to front, matching centers and point A markings.

{veronica day bag}

Sew handle to front. Notch handle seam, and press toward handle.

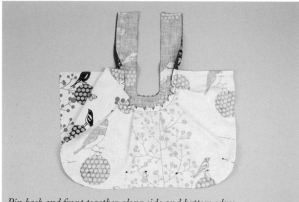

Pin back and front together along side and bottom edges.

3. Stitch the handle to the front from point A to point A, leaving a ½˝ seam allowance at both ends and backtacking at both ends. Notch the curved seam of the handle, and press toward the handle.

4. Repeat Steps 2 and 3 to sew the other handle to the exterior back.

5. Pin the exterior front and back together along the side and bottom edges, with right sides facing.

6. Stitch the side and bottom seams, backtacking at both ends. Notch the curved corner seams.

Making the Pocket

Make the pocket (see Making a Pocket, page 14). Center the pocket on the right side of a lining front or back piece, with the lower (6˝ finished) edge of the pocket placed 3˝ from the bottom edge of the lining. Topstitch the pocket in place—down one side, across the bottom, and back up the other side, backtacking at both ends.

Sewing the Lining

1. Fuse the interfacing to the wrong side of the lining front and back and lining handle pieces.

2. Attach the magnetic snap to the lining front and back pieces as indicated on the pattern (see Adding a Magnetic Snap, page 13).

3. Repeat Steps 2–6 in Sewing the Exterior to complete the lining, leaving 5˝ unstitched along the bottom seam for turning.

Assembling the
Exterior and Lining

1. Press the exterior and lining seams open. Turn the exterior right side out. Insert the exterior inside the lining, with right sides together.

2. Pin the exterior and lining together along the opening edge, from point A on the front, across the side seam, to point A on the back. Pin the other side of the bag in the same manner. Stitch the 2 seams, leaving a ½″ seam allowance and backtacking at both ends. Trim the corners at the tops of the side seams.

3. Pin an exterior handle and a lining handle together from point A to point B. Stitch the seam, backtacking at both ends. Pin along the inside curve of the same handle from point C to point C. Stitch the seam, backtacking at both ends. Clip the curved seam. Repeat for the other handle.

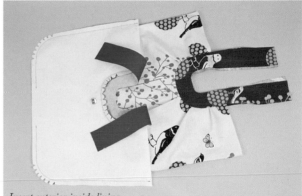

Insert exterior inside lining.

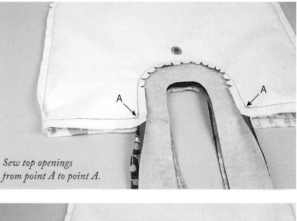

Sew top openings from point A to point A.

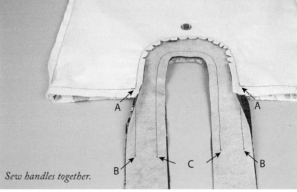

Sew handles together.

Clipping the seams with great care is critical to making this bag a success, especially at the corner where the handle meets the bag at point A. Here, it is a good idea to check the shape of the bag by turning it right side out and making sure the seams are not caught or puckered before you proceed with any final clipping or trimming. By checking first, you can make the job easier if you have to unstitch and sew again.

Check corners before clipping or trimming.

4. Turn the bag right side out through the opening left in the lining. Slipstitch the opening closed. Tuck the lining into the exterior. Press the top opening of the bag.

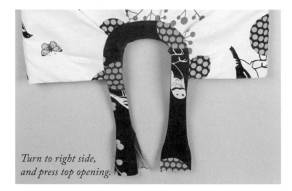

Turn to right side, and press top opening.

Finishing the Bag

1. Pin the short edges of the exterior handles together, right sides facing. Stitch the seams, backtacking at both ends. Press the seams open. Repeat for the lining handles.

2. Turn under ½″ on the raw side edges of the lining and exterior handles, and press. Pin or baste the turned-under edges.

Sew short edges of handles.

3. Topstitch around the opening edge and both sides of the handles, ⅛″ from the edges. The turned-under edges will be secured in the topstitching.

Topstitch opening edge and handles.

79

{veronica day bag}

{ metro shopping bag }

This bag has wide sides and a wide bottom, which allows it to hold a lot. Use a material such as suede for the handle to create a unique look. The lining shows slightly, so it is also important to choose this fabric carefully. You can use either home decorator or quilting-weight cotton fabric.

Use the Metro Shopping Bag Front/Back pattern on pullout page P-4, and the Metro Shopping Bag Side/Bottom pattern on pullout page P-2.

FINISHED SIZE:
approximately 20¼″ × 12″ × 6″, plus 9″ handle

SKILL LEVEL: ●●

WHAT YOU NEED

Fabric amounts are based on 44″-wide fabric.

1¼ yards for exterior

⅛ yard for handles (or 2 pieces of leather or suede 3½″ × 11″)

1¼ yards for lining and pocket

1¾ yards of 22″-wide medium-weight fusible interfacing

18mm magnetic snap

92″ of piping (optional)

4″–5″ of hook-and-loop tape for pocket closure (optional; see Making a Pocket, page 14)

CUTTING THE PIECES

Follow the instructions in Making and Using the Patterns (page 9). Transfer all points and references to the fabric.

exterior

Cut 2 Front/Back pieces.

Cut 2 Side/Bottom pieces.

handles

Cut 2 pieces 3½″ × 11″ for the handles.

lining

Cut 2 Front/Back pieces.

Cut 2 Side/Bottom pieces.

Cut 2 pieces 7″ x 6″ for the pocket.

interfacing

Cut 2 Front/Back pieces.

Cut 2 Side/Bottom pieces.

Sewing the Exterior

1. Fuse the interfacing to the wrong side of the exterior pieces.

2. Pin the side/bottom pieces together along the 7″ edges, right sides together. Stitch the seam, backtacking at both ends. Press the seam open. Topstitch on each side, ⅛″ from the seam, for reinforcement.

3. Pin the front to the assembled side/bottom, with right sides facing. First match the center front with the side/bottom seam and then the point A and point B markings as indicated on the patterns. Clip the side/bottom piece between the A and B markings only as necessary to help ease it around the curve of the front piece.

4. Sew around the bag, backtacking at both ends.

5. Repeat Steps 3 and 4 to attach the back piece to the other side of the assembled side/bottom.

tip -

If you would like to add a sewing label, place it in the desired location. Stitch around the edge, backtacking at the starting/ending point.

- -

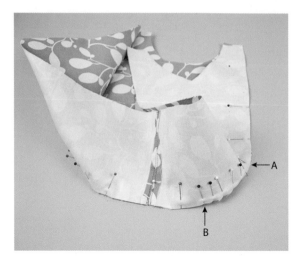

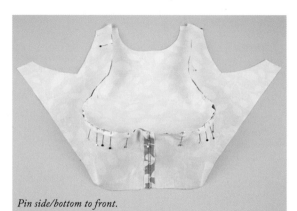

Pin side/bottom to front.

Making the Handles

1. Fold a handle piece in half lengthwise, with the wrong sides together, and press to make a crease. Open the handle with the wrong side facing you. Fold in each side of the handle ½″, and press. Fold in half again along the first crease, and press.

2. Topstitch ⅛″ from both long edges.

3. Repeat for the other handle.

Making the Pocket

Make the pocket (see Making a Pocket, page 14). Center the pocket on the right side of a lining front or back piece, with the lower (6″ finished) edge of the pocket placed 4½″ from the bottom edge of the lining. Topstitch the pocket in place—down one side, across the bottom, and back up the other side, backtacking at both ends.

Sewing the Lining

1. Attach the magnetic snap to the lining front and back pieces as indicated on the pattern (see Adding a Magnetic Snap, page 13).

2. Repeat Steps 2–5 in Sewing the Exterior to complete the lining, leaving 5″ unstitched along a bottom seam for turning.

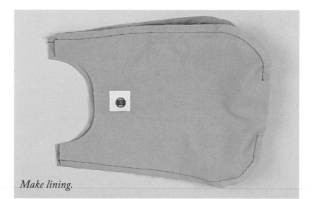

Make lining.

Assembling the Exterior and Lining

1. Press the exterior and lining seams open. Turn the exterior right side out.

2. Position the end of a handle on the right side of the exterior bag front, centered between the C markings as indicated on the pattern. Pin and baste in place. The other end of this handle will be attached later. Pin and baste the remaining handle to the back of the bag in the same manner.

3. Insert the exterior inside the lining, with right sides together, sandwiching the handles between the exterior and the lining.

4. Pin the exterior to the lining around the top opening of the bag.

Attach end of one handle to bag front and end of other handle to bag back.

Insert exterior inside lining.

Pin exterior to lining around top opening.

Leave top opening unstitched between C markings.

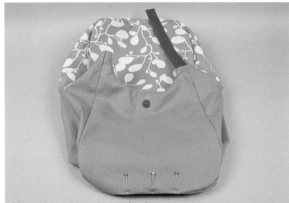

Slipstitch opening in lining closed.

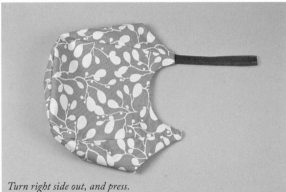

Turn right side out, and press.

Insert handle ends, and pin.

5. Sew around the top opening of the bag, leaving the seams unstitched between the C markings where the remaining handle ends will be inserted. Trim the handle corners and the corners at the tops of the seams. Clip the curved seams.

6. Turn right side out through the opening in the lining. Slipstitch the opening closed.

7. Tuck the lining into the exterior. Press the top opening of the bag.

8. Fold in the ½″ seam allowance of the unstitched handle openings, and press. Insert the remaining handle ends into the handle openings ½″, and pin.

9. Topstitch around the top opening of the bag, ⅛″ from the edge. The inserted handle ends will be secured in the topstitching.

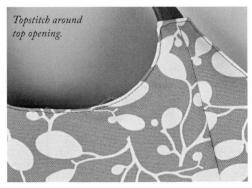

Topstitch around top opening.

{ metro shopping bag }

{ cute elizabeth bag }

This modern bag has a beautiful curved shape and utilizes rings to attach the handle.
It will be very comfortable on your shoulder. The contrasting side pieces give this bag a
designer look. Dress it up even more with a romantic eyelet corsage. You can use either
home decorator or quilting-weight cotton fabric.

*Use the Cute Elizabeth Bag Front/Back pattern on pullout page P-2, the Cute Elizabeth Bag Side/Bottom pattern on
pullout page P-3 and the Floral Bag Petal Template on pullout page P-1.*

FINISHED SIZE: approximately
16½″ × 10¾″ × 3″, plus 12½″ handle

SKILL LEVEL: ●● ○

WHAT YOU NEED

*Fabric amounts are based
on 44″-wide fabric.*

¾ yard for exterior front and back

½ yard for exterior side and
bottom and handles

¾ yard for lining

2 yards of 22″-wide heavyweight
fusible interfacing

4 O-rings, 1¼″ wide, for handles
(round, oval, or rectangular)

18mm magnetic snap

4″–5″ of hook-and-loop tape for
pocket closure (optional; see
Making a Pocket, page 14)

corsage

5½″ × 11″ eyelet fabric

5½″ × 5½″ solid-color fabric

4–5 beads, ½″ in diameter

Invisible thread

CUTTING THE PIECES

Follow the instructions in Making and Using the Patterns (page 9). Transfer all points and references to the fabric.

exterior

Cut 2 Front/Back pieces.

Cut 1 Side/Bottom piece.

Cut 2 pieces 3½˝ × 14˝ for the handles.

lining

Cut 2 Front/Back pieces.

Cut 1 Side/Bottom piece.

Cut 2 pieces 7˝ × 6˝ for the pocket.

interfacing

Cut 2 Front/Back pieces.

Cut 1 Side/Bottom piece.

corsage

Cut 2 petals from the eyelet fabric.

Cut 1 petal from the solid-color fabric.

Sewing the Exterior

1. Fuse the interfacing to the wrong side of the exterior front, back, and side/bottom pieces.

2. Pin the front piece to the side/bottom piece, with right sides facing. Match the centers and then the point A and point B markings as indicated on the patterns. Clip the side/bottom piece between the A and B markings only as necessary to help ease it around the curve of the front piece.

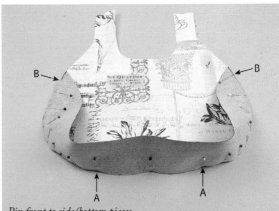

Pin front to side/bottom pieces.

Sew front to side/bottom between point B markings, backtacking at each end.

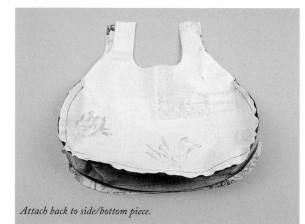

Attach back to side/bottom piece.

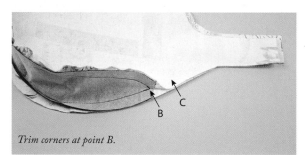

Trim corners at point B.

3. Sew the seam just to point B, backtacking at each end.

4. Repeat Steps 2–3 to attach the back piece to the other side of the side/bottom piece. Trim the corners, and notch the curved seams.

5. After sewing the front and back pieces to the side/bottom piece, stitch from points B to C on each side, backtacking at both ends.

Making the Pocket

Make the pocket (see Making a Pocket, page 14). Center the pocket on the right side of a lining front or back piece, with the lower (6″ finished) edge of the pocket placed 3¾″ from the bottom edge of the lining. Topstitch the pocket in place—down one side, across the bottom, and back up the other side, back-tacking at both ends.

Sewing the Lining

1. Attach the magnetic snap to the lining front and back pieces as indicated on the pattern (see Adding a Magnetic Snap, page 13).

2. Repeat Steps 2–5 in Sewing the Exterior to complete the lining, leaving 5″ unstitched along a bottom seam for turning.

Assembling the Exterior and Lining

1. Press the exterior and lining seams open. Turn the exterior right side out.

2. Insert the exterior inside the lining, with right sides together.

3. Pin the exterior and the lining together around the top opening, including the handle extensions, from point C on one side to point C on the other side. Pin the other side of the bag in the same manner.

4. Sew around the top opening of the bag, including the handle extensions, from point C on one side to point C on the other side, carefully pivoting at the corners of the handle extensions and backtacking at both ends. Sew the other side of the bag in the same manner.

5. Trim the corner seam allowances on all 4 handle extensions.

6. Clip and notch the curved seams. Turn the bag and handle extensions right side out through the opening left in the lining. Carefully push out the corners of the handles. Stitch the opening closed.

7. Tuck the lining into the exterior. Press the top opening of the bag, including the handle extensions.

8. Topstitch around the top opening, ⅛″ from the edge.

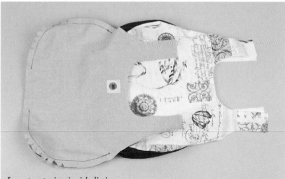

Insert exterior inside lining.

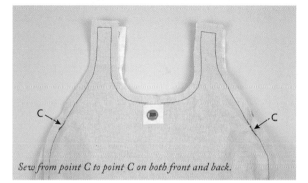

Sew from point C to point C on both front and back.

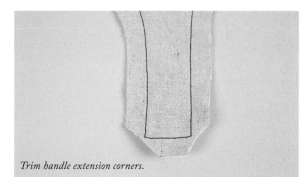

Trim handle extension corners.

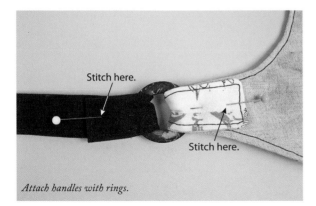

Stitch here.

Stitch here.

Attach handles with rings.

Making the Handles

1. Fold in ½″ along both short edges of a handle piece, and press. Fold the handle piece in half lengthwise, with the wrong sides together, and press to make a crease. Open the handle with the wrong side facing you. Fold in each side of the handle ½″, and press. Fold in half again along the first crease, and press. Topstitch ⅛″ from both long edges. Repeat for the other handle.

2. To attach the handle rings: slip a handle extension through a ring, and fold the extension over 1″ to the lining side. Pin in place. Repeat with the other 3 rings.

3. To attach the handles: slip the end of a handle through a ring on the bag front. Fold the end over 1″ to the lining side, and pin in place. Pin the other handle end to the other front extension. Pin the remaining handle to the bag back extensions in the same manner.

4. Stitch the extension and handle ends in place, close to the short ends.

Sew running stitch circles in centers of petals.

Making the Corsage

Draw a 1″ circle in the center of each of the 2 eyelet petals; draw a 2″ circle on the solid fabric petal. Stitch around the circle using a running stitch, and pull the thread to gather. Layer the petals as shown, and stitch together through all the layers. Sew the beads to the center using invisible thread. Attach to bag where desired.

Sew petals together through center. Sew beads to center.

{ cute elizabeth bag }

{urban carryall bag}

You'll be able to put anything and everything in this shapely bag! An added zipper will prevent things from falling out, and the bias binding used to finish the lining will give the bag extra body. Fabrics with large prints are a great choice. You can use either home decorator or quilting-weight cotton fabric.

Use the Urban Carryall Exterior Front Top, the Urban Carryall Exterior Front Pleats Panel, and the Urban Carryall Lining Front/Back and Exterior Back Corner patterns on pullout page P-4.

FINISHED SIZE: 22¾″ × 15″, plus adjustable handle, approximately 10″ folded

SKILL LEVEL: ●●○

WHAT YOU NEED

Fabric amounts are based on 44″-wide fabric.

1¼ yards for exterior

1⅛ yards for lining

¼ yard for lining binding (to make your own bias binding, see page 16)

OR 57″ of ½″-wide double-fold bias tape (purchased)

19″ all-purpose zipper

3″ O-ring for handle (round, oval, or rectangular)

4″–5″ of hook-and-loop tape for pocket closure (optional; see Making a Pocket, page 14)

CUTTING THE PIECES

Follow the instructions in Making and Using the Patterns (page 9). Cut the rectangular and square pieces first, and then cut the pattern pieces as required. Transfer all points and references to the fabric.

exterior

Cut 2 pieces 20″ × 2″ for the zipper panels.

Cut 1 piece 6″ × 35″ for the handle.

Cut 1 piece 6″ × 6″ for the loop

Cut 1 piece 24″ × 16″ for the back. Refer to the Front/Back diagram to mark the pieces and to trace and trim the corners using the Urban Carryall Lining Front/Back and Exterior Back Corner pattern.

Cut 1 Front Top piece.

Cut 1 Front Pleats Panel piece.

lining

Cut 2 pieces 24″ × 16″ for the front and back. Refer to the Front/Back diagram to mark the pieces and to trace and trim the corners using the Urban Carryall Lining Front/Back and Exterior Back Corner pattern.

Cut 2 pieces 20″ × 2″ for the zipper panels.

Cut 2 pieces 7″ × 7″ for the pockets.

lining binding

Refer to Making Bias Binding, page 16, to make 57″ of bias binding, or use purchased binding.

Cut 1 piece 48″ long.

Cut 2 pieces 4½″ long each.

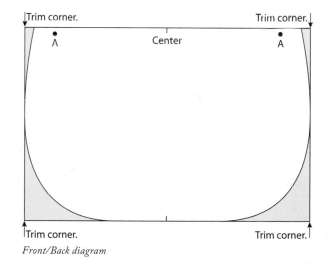

Front/Back diagram

Making the Pocket

Make the pocket (see Making a Pocket, page 14). Center the pocket on the right side of a lining front or back piece, with the lower edge of the pocket placed 5½″ from the bottom edge of the lining. Topstitch the pocket in place—down one side, across the bottom, and back up the other side, backtacking at both ends.

Sewing the Exterior and Lining

1. Make the pleats on the exterior front pleats panel (see Sewing Darts and Pleats, page 16). Make sure the pleats on both sides fold *away from* the center.

2. Pin the exterior front top piece to the exterior front pleats panel, with right sides facing and matching the centers. Stitch the seam, backtacking at both ends. Notch the curved seam of the exterior front top.

3. Press the seam toward the exterior front top. Topstitch the exterior front top, ⅛″ from the seam.

4. Center an exterior zipper panel piece over the A markings on the top edge of the front, and pin in place. The zipper panel will extend ½″ beyond the A markings on each side. Stitch the zipper panel to the front top between the A markings only, backtacking at each end. Press the seam toward the zipper panel.

5. Topstitch the zipper panel between the A markings only, ⅛″ from the seam, backtacking at both ends. The ½″ extension will be left at each end.

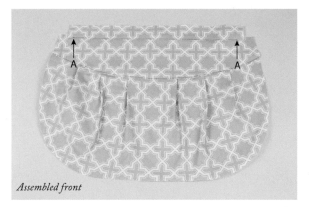

Assembled front

6. Repeat Steps 4 and 5 to stitch the other exterior zipper panel piece to the exterior back piece in the same manner.

7. Repeat Steps 4 and 5 to sew the lining zipper panel pieces to the lining front and lining back pieces in the same manner.

Installing the Zipper

1. Referring to the photo at right, close the zipper and place it on the exterior front zipper panel with right sides together. Position the zipper pull ⅝″ from the side edge of the zipper panel, and then align the edge of the zipper tape along the raw upper edge of the zipper panel. Trim excess zipper tape from the opposite side edge, but not closer than ¼″ from the zipper stop. If you need to trim away more of the zipper, see Shortening Zipper Length (page 12).

2. Pin the zipper to the exterior zipper panel.

3. Using a zipper foot, stitch the zipper to the top panel ⅛″ from the edge of the tape, backtacking at both ends.

4. Align the raw edge of the lining front zipper panel with the raw edge of the exterior front zipper panel, with right sides together, and pin. The zipper will now be sandwiched between the lining and the exterior.

5. Using a zipper foot, sew the 3 layers together, close to the zipper coils, backtacking at both ends.

6. Flip the lining over to the wrong side, and press. From the exterior side, topstitch the zipper panel close to the zipper coils.

7. Attach the exterior back and lining back in the same manner.

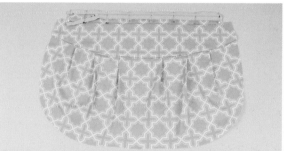

Pin zipper to exterior zipper panel.

Pin lining front to top panel, with zipper in between.

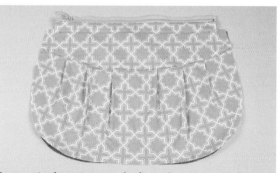

Sew exterior front zipper panel to lining front zipper panel, turn, and press.

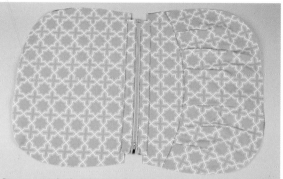

Sew exterior back zipper panel to lining back zipper panel, turn, and press.

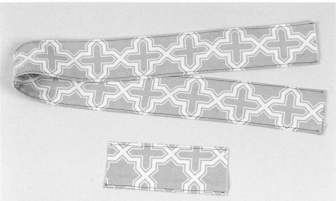

Make handle and loop.

Assembled O-ring

Making the Handle and Loop

1. Fold in ½″ along a short edge of the long handle piece, and press.

2. Fold the handle in half length-wise, with the wrong sides together, and press to make a crease. Open the handle with the wrong side facing you. Fold in each side of the handle ½″, and press. Fold in half again along the first crease, and press. Topstitch ⅛″ from both long edges. Set aside.

3. Repeat Step 2 to make the loop.

4. Insert an end of the loop through the O-ring, and fold the loop in half, wrong sides together.

5. Baste the raw ends of the loop together ¼″ from the edge to keep the O-ring from slipping out.

Assembling the Exterior and Lining

1. Baste the exterior front and lining front together around the outside edge, ½″ from the edge. Trim the seam allowances to ⅜″, and treat the 2 layers as 1. Repeat for the back. Open the zipper, so that you can turn the bag right side out later. Pin the front and back together through all 4 layers, with right (exterior) sides facing. If desired, baste around the outside edge to hold everything in place.

2. Unfold the 48″ length of bias binding. Beginning at the outside corner on a side of the bag, pin the raw edge of the bias binding to the outside edge of the bag, with right sides together. Pin all the way around to the other outside corner on the other side. Trim any excess binding even with the outside corner.

3. Stitch along the crease line closest to the outside edge. Fold the binding over to encase the raw edge, and pin.

4. Topstitch the binding ⅛″ from the inner fold of the binding, through all the layers.

5. With the bag still inside out and the zipper open, center the assembled loop over a side seam with right sides together (fold the lining binding to one side), and pin. Fold the zipper panels over to cover the loop, with the zipper coils meeting in the center.

6. Stitch across the seam, sewing back and forth several times to reinforce. Trim the seam allowances to ⅜″.

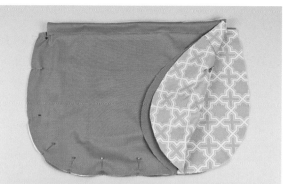

Pin front and back together through all 4 layers, with exterior sides facing.

Pin binding around outside edge.

Fold binding over to encase raw edge, and pin.

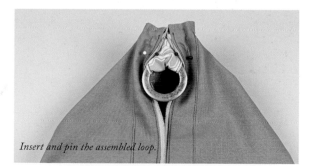

Insert and pin the assembled loop.

{ urban carryall bag }

Stitch binding to trimmed seam.

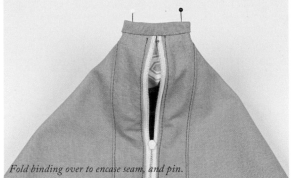
Fold binding over to encase seam, and pin.

Adjust handle, and stitch to secure.

7. Unfold a 4½″ length of bias binding. Center the binding over the trimmed seam, and pin the raw edge of the bias binding in place, with right sides together. Stitch along the crease line closest to the edge of the trimmed seam, backtacking at both ends.

8. Fold in the ends of the binding, so they are even with the ends of the seam. Fold the binding over to encase the raw edge, and pin.

9. Topstitch the binding ⅛″ from the inner fold of the binding, through all the layers.

10. Insert the unfinished end of the long handle at the other end of the bag in the same manner. Turn the bag right side out.

Finishing the Bag

Insert the finished end of the long handle through the O-ring. Pull the handle to the desired length. Pin and stitch the end of the handle ⅛″ from the edge.

99

{ urban carryall bag }

{sweet annemarie bag}

This bag is the perfect size for carrying a wallet and cell phone, and because it is a cross-body style of bag (the strap crosses the body from one shoulder to the opposite hip), it is appropriate for active days requiring lots of movement. Add the corsage if you wish. You can use either home decorator or quilting-weight cotton fabric.

Use the Sweet Annemarie Bag Front/Back and the Sweet Annemarie Bag Flap patterns on pullout page P-4.

FINISHED SIZE:
approximately 11″ × 7⅛″, plus 19″ handle

SKILL LEVEL: ●●

WHAT YOU NEED

Fabric amounts are based on 44″-wide fabric.

½ yard for exterior

⅜ yard for lining

¼ yard for corsage (optional)

⅝ yard of 22″-wide heavyweight iron-on fusible interfacing

18mm magnetic snap

1½″ O-ring for handle (round, oval, or rectangular)

1½″–2″ bead or button

¾″–1″ button for corsage (optional)

CUTTING THE PIECES

Follow the instructions in Making and Using the Patterns (page 9). Transfer all points and references to the fabric.

exterior

Cut 2 Front/Back pieces.

Cut 1 Flap piece.

Cut 1 piece 2˝ × 40½˝ for the strap.

Cut 1 piece 2˝ × 3½˝ for the ring loop.

lining

Cut 2 Front/Back pieces.

Cut 1 Flap piece.

interfacing

Cut 2 Front/Back pieces.

Cut 1 Flap piece.

corsage

Cut 1 circle 5¾˝ in diameter.

Cut 1 circle 5˝ in diameter.

Cut 1 circle 4½˝ in diameter.

Cut 1 circle 4˝ in diameter.

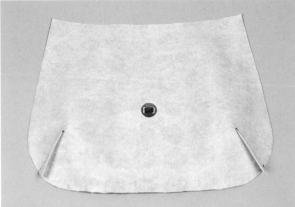
Sew front and back darts, and press.

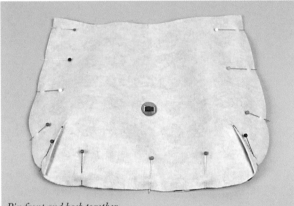
Pin front and back together.

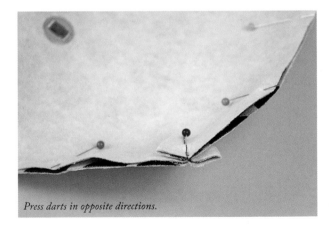
Press darts in opposite directions.

Sewing the Exterior and Lining

1. Fuse the interfacing to the wrong side of the exterior front, back, and flap pieces.

2. Attach the magnetic snap to the exterior front and lining flap pieces as indicated on the patterns (see Adding a Magnetic Snap, page 13).

3. Sew the darts on the exterior front and back pieces (see Sewing Darts and Pleats, page 16). Press the darts on the front piece toward the center. Press the darts on the back piece toward the outside edge.

✤note✤ To help suede or leather darts lie flat, clip each one along the fold of the dart, close to, but not through, the point. Finger-press the darts open, and then topstitch around the dart seams from the right side, ⅛″ from the seams.

4. Pin the front and back exterior pieces around the side and bottom edges, with the right sides together. The darts on the front and back pieces will be pressed in opposite directions, so they will lie flat.

5. Sew around the side and bottom edges, backtacking at both ends. Notch the curved seam.

6. Repeat Steps 3–5 with the lining pieces, leaving 4″ unstitched along the bottom edge for turning.

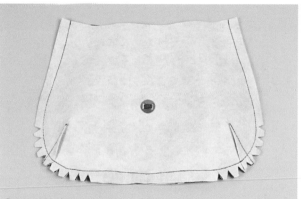
Sew and notch curved seam.

Sew lining, leaving 4″ unstitched.

Making the Strap and Ring Loop

1. Fold in ½″ on a short edge of the strap piece, and press.

2. Fold the strap in half lengthwise, with the wrong sides together, and press to make a crease. Open the strap with the wrong side facing you. Fold in each side of the strap ½″, and press. Fold in half again along the first crease, and press. Topstitch ⅛″ from the folded-in edges.

Topstitch ⅛″ from folded-in edges.

3. Repeat Step 2 to make the ring loop. Insert an end of the ring loop through the O-ring, and fold the loop in half. Pin the raw ends of the loop together to keep the O-ring from slipping out.

Make ring loop.

Topstitch flap.

Making the Flap

1. Pin the exterior flap and lining flap together with right sides facing. Stitch only the curved seam, leaving the straight edge unstitched. Notch the curved seam, and trim the seam allowance to ¼″.

2. Turn the flap right side out, and press. Topstitch ⅛″ from the seam.

Pin and baste ring loop.

Assembling the Exterior and Lining

1. Press the exterior and lining seams open. Turn the exterior right side out.

2. Center the raw ends of the ring loop over an exterior side seam, with right sides together. Pin and baste in place.

3. Center the raw end of the strap over the other exterior side seam, with right sides together. Pin and baste in place.

Pin and baste strap.

4. Center the flap on the back of the bag, with the exterior sides together, aligning the raw edges. Pin and baste in place.

5. Insert the exterior inside the lining, right sides together. The flap, strap, and ring loop should all be sandwiched between the lining and the exterior.

6. Pin the exterior and lining together around the opening of the bag.

Pin and baste flap.

Insert exterior inside lining.

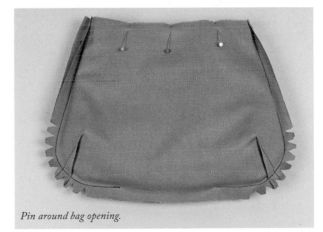

Pin around bag opening.

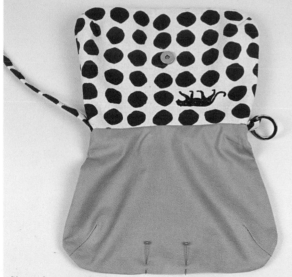

7. Stitch around the opening of the bag, taking care not to catch the strap in the seam. Trim the corners at the tops of the seams. Clip the seam. Turn right side out through the opening left in the lining. Slipstitch the opening closed.

8. Tuck the lining into the exterior. Press the top opening of the bag. Topstitch around the opening, ⅛″ from the edge. Sew the bead or button to the exterior flap in the desired location.

Slipstitch opening closed.

Connect strap.

Connecting the Strap

From the right side, insert the finished end of the strap into the O-ring. Fold the end under to make a 1″ loop. Stitch across the end of the strap, sewing back and forth several times to reinforce.

Stitch darts ½″ long and ¼″ deep from centers of circles.

Making the Corsage

1. Fold a petal circle in half, right sides together. From the center of the circle, stitch a dart approximately ¼″ deep and approximately ½″ long toward the outside edge of the circle. Repeat with the 3 remaining petal circles.

2. Open the petals. With the right sides facing up, align the darts and layer the petals, largest on the bottom. Sew the 4 petals together through the center.

3. Sew the button to the center of the petals.

4. Sew the corsage to the center of the flap.

Layer petals, and sew together.

{ sweet annemarie bag }

{ floral bag }

The corsage and pleats give this bag a stylish look. It can be carried with casual attire or matched with a formal style of dress. Small prints work well on this bag. Try mixing different fabrics and colors to make the corsage: eyelet, silk (dupioni), lace, or wool. The large version of this bag has shorter handles than the small version, due to their differences in the size. You can use either home decorator or quilting-weight cotton fabric for this bag.

Use the Floral Bag Bottom Corner and the Floral Bag Corsage Petal patterns on pullout page P-1.

FINISHED SIZE: 20″ × 18″, plus 12¼″ handle (large), or 16″ × 14″, plus 13¼″ handle (small)

SKILL LEVEL: ●●

WHAT YOU NEED

Fabric amounts are based on 44″-wide fabric.

large
- 1½ yards for exterior
- 1⅛ yards for lining
- ½ yard for corsage
- 2 yards of 22″-wide lightweight fusible interfacing
- 18mm magnetic snap
- 80″ of leather cording for corsage
- 1 brooch pin for corsage
- Glue gun and glue

small
- 1 yard for exterior
- ⅞ yard for lining
- ½ yard for corsage
- 1½ yards of 22″-wide lightweight fusible interfacing
- 18mm magnetic snap
- 80″ of leather cording for corsage
- 1 brooch pin for corsage
- Glue gun and glue

CUTTING THE PIECES

Follow the instructions in Making and Using the Patterns (page 9). Transfer all points and references to the fabric.

large

exterior

Cut 2 pieces 30″ × 15″ for the front and back. Refer to the Front and Back diagram to mark the pieces and to trace and trim the bottom corners using the Floral Bag Bottom Corner template.

Cut 2 pieces 21″ × 5″ for the front and back top panels. Refer to the Top Panel diagram to mark the pieces.

Cut 2 pieces 6½″ × 25½″ for the handles.

lining

Cut 2 pieces 30″ × 15″ for the front and back. Refer to the Front and Back diagram to mark the pieces and to trace and trim the bottom corners using the Floral Bag Bottom Corner template.

Cut 2 pieces 21″ × 5″ for the front and back top panels. Refer to the Top Panel diagram to mark the pieces.

interfacing

Cut 2 pieces 30″ × 15″ for the front and back. Refer to the Front and Back diagram to mark the pieces and to trace and trim the bottom corners using the Floral Bag Bottom Corner template.

Cut 2 pieces 21″ × 5″ for the front and back top panels. Refer to the Top Panel diagram to mark the pieces.

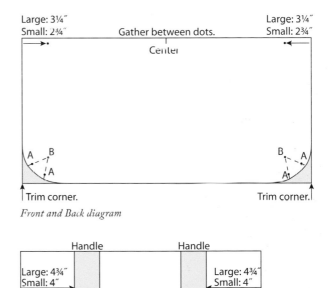

Large: 3¼″
Small: 2¾″ — Gather between dots. — Large: 3¼″ Small: 2¾″

Center

A — B — A · A — B — A

Trim corner. — Trim corner.

Front and Back diagram

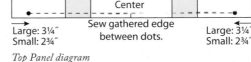

Handle — Handle

Large: 4¾″ Small: 4″ — Center — Large: 4¾″ Small: 4″

Large: 3¼″ Small: 2¾″ — Sew gathered edge between dots. — Large: 3¼″ Small: 2¾″

Top Panel diagram

exterior

Cut 2 pieces 23½″ × 12″ for the front and back. Refer to the Front and Back diagram to mark the pieces and to trace and trim the bottom corners using the Floral Bag Bottom Corner template.

Cut 2 pieces 17″ × 4″ for the front and back top panels. Refer to the Top Panel diagram to mark the pieces.

Cut 2 pieces 4½″ × 27½″ for the handles.

lining

Cut 2 pieces 23½″ × 12″ for the front and back. Refer to the Front and Back diagram to mark the pieces and to trace and trim the bottom corners using the Floral Bag Bottom Corner template.

Cut 2 pieces 17″ × 4″ for the front and back top panels. Refer to the Top Panel diagram to mark the pieces.

interfacing

Cut 2 pieces 23½″ × 12″ for the front and back. Refer to the Front and Back diagram to mark the pieces and to trace and trim the bottom corners using the Floral Bag Bottom Corner template.

Cut 2 pieces 17″ × 4″ for the front and back top panels. Refer to the Top Panel diagram to mark the pieces.

corsage

Cut 13 petal pieces.

tip

You can change the number of petals in your corsage depending on the thickness of the material. If the material is thick or heavy, such as linen or wool, use fewer than 12 petals. For thin materials such as eyelet or lace, 18–22 petals should give a rich, elegant look.

Making the Handles

1. Fold a handle piece in half lengthwise, with the wrong sides together, and press to make a crease. Open the handle with the wrong side facing you. Fold in each side of the handle ½″, and press. Fold in half again along the first crease, and press. Topstitch ⅛″ away from both sides.

2. Fuse the interfacing to the wrong side of the exterior top panels and the exterior front and back.

3. Position the handle on an exterior top panel piece as marked, with right sides facing, aligning the raw edges of the handle with the bottom edge of the top panel. Baste the handle in place.

4. Repeat with the remaining handle and top panel piece.

Baste handles to top panels.

✤ note ✤ Several of the bags in this book have the handle positioned at the top edge of the bag, rather than in the lower seam of the top panel. If you prefer to have the handles attached at the top edge of the bag, you can baste the handles in place just after Step 1 in Assembling the Exterior and Lining. You also can hand sew the handles to the top panel after completing the bag or attach them with finished ends to the top panels using small buttons.

Sewing the Exterior

1. Sew the darts on the exterior front and back pieces (see Sewing Darts and Pleats, page 16). Press the darts on the front piece toward the center. Press the darts on the back piece toward the outside edge.

2. To gather the front and back pieces along the top edge, lengthen your sewing machine stitch length slightly, and sew 2 rows between the dots as marked on the Front and Back diagram. Stitch the first row just inside the ½″ line, and stitch the second row within the seam allowance, ⅛″ away. Do not backtack, and leave long thread ends for gathering.

3. Pin a top panel and the front piece together, with right sides facing. Pin from each side edge to the beginning of the gathering stitching, and then match and pin the marked centers. Pull the top threads on each side to gather and adjust the length to match up with the top panel. Wind the threads around the pins in a figure-eight pattern to hold the gathers. Pin the rest of the top panel, arranging the gathers evenly.

4. Sew the front and top panel together, backtacking at both ends. Remove the gathering threads.

Sew front and back darts, and press.

Pin front to top panel, and gather to fit.

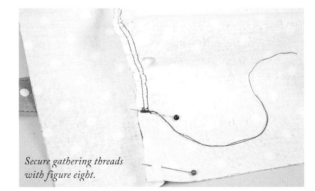

Secure gathering threads with figure eight.

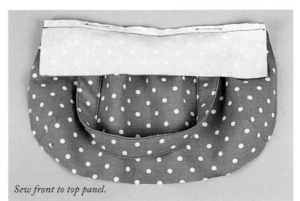

Sew front to top panel.

Press and topstitch top panel.

Pin front and back together.

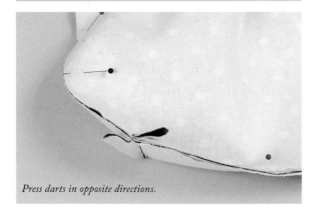

Press darts in opposite directions.

5. Press the seam toward the top panel. Press the handle up toward the top panel. Topstitch along the top panel, ⅛˝ from the edge, stitching over the handle.

6. Repeat Steps 3–5 for the back piece and the remaining top panel.

7. Pin the assembled front and back exterior pieces with the right sides together. The darts on the front and back pieces will be pressed in opposite directions, so they will lie flat.

8. Sew around the side and bottom edges, backtacking at both ends. Notch the curved seam.

Sewing the Lining

1. Attach the magnetic snap to the lining front and back pieces as marked (see Adding a Magnetic Snap, page 13).

2. Repeat Steps 1–8 in Sewing the Exterior, leaving 5˝ unstitched along the bottom edge for turning.

Assembling the Exterior and Lining

1. Press the exterior and lining side seams open. Turn the exterior right side out.

2. Insert the exterior inside the lining, with right sides together.

3. Pin the exterior and lining together around the top opening of the bag.

4. Stitch around the top opening of the bag. Trim the corners at the tops of the seams. Turn right side out through the opening left in the lining. Slipstitch the opening closed.

5. Tuck the lining into the exterior. Press the top opening of the bag. Move the handles out of the way, and topstitch around the opening ⅛″ from the edge.

Insert exterior inside lining.

Pin around opening.

Slipstitch opening closed.

Fold 12 petals into eighths.

Making the Corsage

1. Fold 12 petals into eighths as shown in the photo.

2. Place the 13th petal right side up as a base layer. Arrange each of the 12 folded petals on the base petal, with the folded points in the center. Sew the folded points of each petal in place. Do not iron the petals, or your corsage will be flat.

3. Cut the leather cord into 4 pieces, each 20″ long. Fold the cords in half. Sew the folds of the cords to the center back of the corsage.

4. Using the glue gun, attach the brooch pin above the leather cords.

5. Attach the corsage to the bag.

Sew petal points to center of base petal.

Sew cords, and glue brooch pin to back.

{floral bag}

{ easy lazy bag }

Do you have those days when you want to sew but you don't have a lot of time? Then this is the bag for you—there's only one pattern piece. It's the perfect lazy Saturday afternoon project! You can use either home decorator or quilting-weight cotton fabric.

Use the Easy Lazy Bag Front/Back: 1 and the Easy Lazy Bag Front/Back: 2 patterns on pullout page P-3. Join them together as indicated to make one pattern piece.

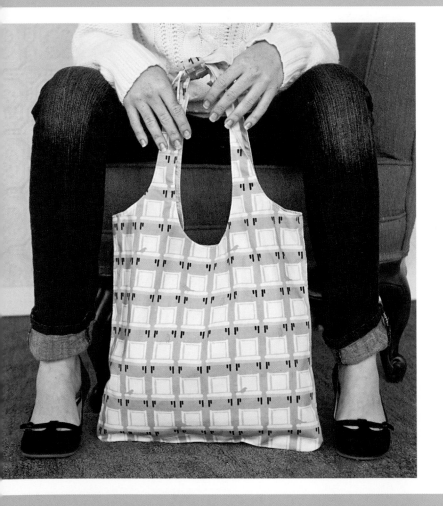

FINISHED SIZE:
approximately 14″ × 14″, plus 10″ handles (tied)

SKILL LEVEL: ◑

WHAT YOU NEED

Fabric amounts are based on 44″-wide fabric.

1 yard for exterior

1 yard for lining

1¾ yards of 22″-wide lightweight fusible interfacing (optional)

18mm magnetic snap

4″–5″ of hook-and-loop tape for pocket closure (optional; see Making a Pocket, page 14)

CUTTING THE PIECES

Follow the instructions in Making and Using the Patterns (page 9). Transfer all points and references to the fabric.

exterior

Cut 2 Front/Back pieces.

lining

Cut 2 Front/Back pieces.

Cut 2 pieces 7″ × 7″ for the pocket.

interfacing (optional)

Cut 2 Front/Back pieces.

Making the Pocket

Make the pocket (see Making a Pocket, page 14). Center the pocket on the right side of a lining front or back piece, with the lower edge of the pocket placed 3½″ from the bottom edge of the lining. Topstitch the pocket in place—down one side, across the bottom, and back up the other side, backtacking at both ends.

Sewing the Exterior and Lining

1. If you choose to use interfacing, fuse it to the wrong side of the exterior front and back pieces.

2. Pin the exterior front and back pieces around the side and bottom edges, with right sides together.

3. Sew around the side and bottom edges, backtacking at both ends. Notch the rounded corner seams.

4. Attach the magnetic snap to the lining front and back pieces as indicated on the pattern (see Adding a Magnetic Snap, page 13).

5. Repeat Steps 2 and 3 with the lining front and back pieces, leaving 5″ unstitched along the bottom edge for turning.

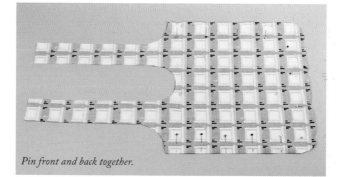

Pin front and back together.

Assembling the Exterior and Lining

1. Press the exterior and lining seams open. Turn the exterior right side out. Insert the exterior inside the lining, with right sides together.

2. Pin the exterior and the lining together all around the top opening, including the 4 handles.

3. Sew around the top opening, including across the ends of each of the 4 handles, carefully pivoting at the corners.

4. Trim the corners at the ends of the handles and at the tops of the side seams. Clip the curved seams.

5. Turn the bag right side out through the opening left in the lining. Push out the handle corners. Slipstitch the opening closed.

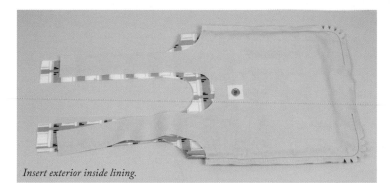

Insert exterior inside lining.

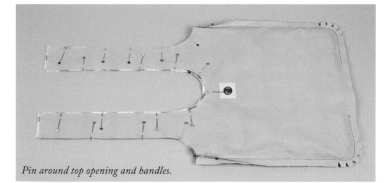

Pin around top opening and handles.

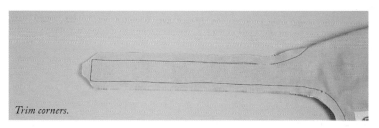

Trim corners.

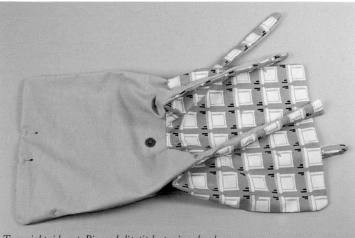

Turn right side out. Pin and slipstitch opening closed.

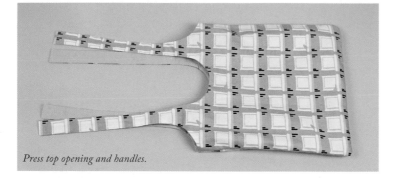

Press top opening and handles.

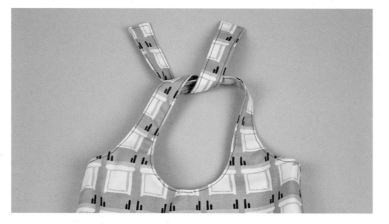

6. Tuck the lining into the exterior. Press the top opening of the bag, including the handles.

7. Topstitch around the top opening and handles, ⅛″ from the edge. Tie the ends of the handles twice to form a knot.

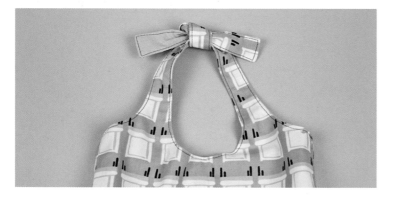

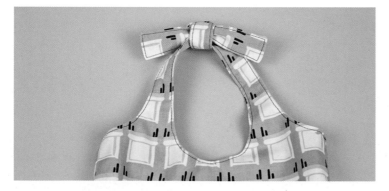

{ elva bag }

This bag has wide bottom and side panels that extend to become the handles, giving it a nice shape. Consider using suede for the side/bottom and flap pieces to make your bag look professional. Mix and match coordinating fabrics for the exterior, lining, sides, bottom, and handles. You can use either home decorator or quilting-weight cotton fabric.

Use the Elva Bag Front/Back, the Elva Bag Side/Bottom, and the Elva Bag Flap Corner patterns on pullout page P–3.

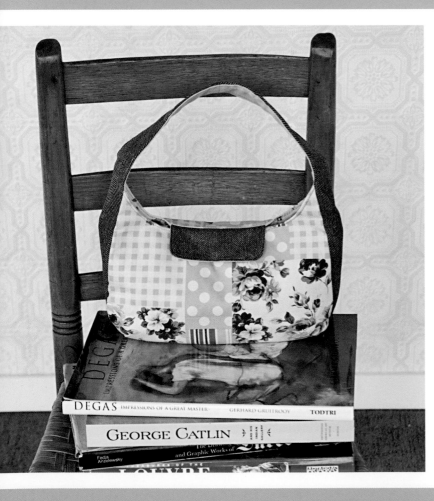

FINISHED SIZE:
11″ × 6½″ × 3″, plus 7″ handle (folded)

SKILL LEVEL: ●●

WHAT YOU NEED

Fabric amounts are based on 44″-wide fabric.

½ yard or pieces sewn together to equal ½ yard for exterior front and back

¼ yard for exterior side/bottom pieces and flap

⅝ yard for lining

1 yard of 22″-wide heavyweight fusible interfacing

18mm magnetic snap

4″–5″ of hook-and-loop tape for pocket closure (optional; see Making a Pocket, page 14)

CUTTING THE PIECES

Follow the instructions in Making and Using the Patterns (page 9). Transfer all points and references to the fabric.

exterior

Cut 2 Front/Back pieces.

Cut 2 Side/Bottom pieces.

Cut 1 piece 5½″ × 2⅝″ for the flap. Refer to the Bag Flap diagram to mark the pieces and to trace and trim the bottom corners using the Elva Bag Flap Corner template.

lining

Cut 2 Front/Back pieces.

Cut 2 Side/Bottom pieces.

Cut 1 piece 5½″ × 2⅝″ for the flap. Refer to the Bag Flap diagram to mark the pieces and to trace and trim the bottom corners using the Elva Bag Flap Corner template.

Cut 2 pieces 5″ × 4″ for the pocket.

interfacing

Cut 2 Front/Back pieces.

Cut 2 Side/Bottom pieces.

Cut 1 piece 2⅝″ × 5½″ for the flap. Refer to the Bag Flap diagram to mark the pieces and to trace and trim the bottom corners using the Elva Bag Flap Corner template.

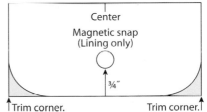

Bag Flap diagram

Making the Pocket

Make the pocket (see Making a Pocket, page 14). Center the pocket on the right side of a lining front or back piece, with the lower (4″ finished) edge of the pocket placed 2¼″ from the bottom edge of the lining. Topstitch the pocket in place—down one side, across the bottom, and back up the other side, backtacking at both ends.

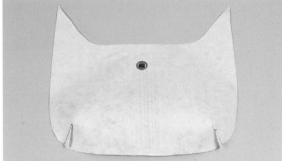

Sew front and back darts, and press.

Stitch side/bottom pieces together along 4″ edges.

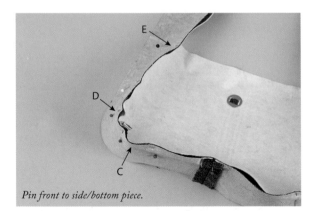

E
D
C

Pin front to side/bottom piece.

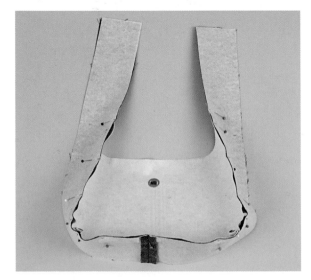

Sewing the Exterior

1. Fuse the interfacing to the wrong side of the exterior pieces.

2. Attach half of the magnetic snap to the exterior front piece as indicated on the pattern (see Adding a Magnetic Snap, page 13). The other half will be attached to the lining flap later.

3. Sew the darts on the exterior front and back pieces (see Sewing Darts and Pleats, page 16). Press the darts on the front piece toward the center. Press the darts on the back piece toward the outside edge.

4. Pin the side/bottom pieces together along the 4″ edges, right sides together. Stitch the seam, backtacking at each end. Press the seam open. Topstitch on each side, ⅛″ from the seam, for reinforcement.

5. Pin the front piece to the assembled side/bottom pieces, with right sides facing. First match the center front with the side/bottom seam, then the point C and point D markings as indicated on the patterns, and finally the point E markings. Clip the side/bottom piece between the C and D markings only as necessary to help ease it around the curve of the front piece.

6. Sew the side and bottom seam, backtacking at both ends.

7. Repeat Steps 5 and 6 to attach the back piece to the other side of the assembled side/bottom piece.

8. Repeat Steps 3–7 to complete the lining, leaving 4″ unstitched along a bottom seam for turning.

Making the Flap

1. Cut the slots for the magnetic snap placement on the flap lining piece (see Adding a Magnetic Snap, page 13).

2. Pin the exterior flap to the lining flap, with right sides facing. Stitch the side and bottom seams, leaving the top straight edge unstitched. Notch the curved seam, and trim the seam allowance to ¼˝.

3. Turn the flap right side out. Press, and topstitch ⅛˝ from the seam.

4. Attach the other half of the magnetic snap (see Adding a Magnetic Snap, page 13) on the lining of the flap.

Assembling the Exterior and Lining

1. Press the exterior and lining seams open. Turn the exterior right side out.

2. Center the flap on the back piece of the bag, with the exterior sides together, aligning the raw edges. Pin and baste in place.

3. Insert the exterior into the lining, right sides together, with the flap sandwiched between the layers.

4. Pin the exterior and the lining together across the front top opening, from point E on one side to point E on the other side. Pin the back of the bag in the same manner.

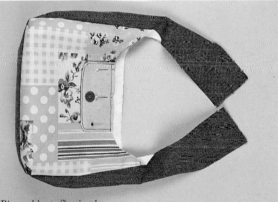

Pin and baste flap in place.

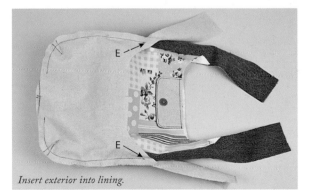

Insert exterior into lining.

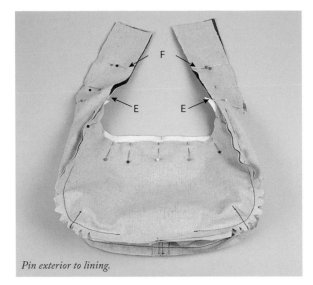

Pin exterior to lining.

5. Pin the exterior and the lining side/bottom together from point E to point F on all 4 sides to make the handles.

6. Stitch the seams in sections, backtacking at the ends of each section. First stitch from points E to E on the front and back and then from points E to F on the sides of each handle. Trim the corners at the tops of the seams (point E).

7. Turn the bag and handles right side out through the opening left in the lining. Push out the handles. Stitch the opening closed. Tuck the lining into the exterior. Press the top opening of the bag, including the handles.

Sew short edges of handles.

Finishing the Bag

1. Pin the short edges of the exterior handles together, right sides facing. Stitch the seams, backtacking at both ends. Press the seams open. Repeat for the lining handles.

2. Turn under ½″ on the raw side edges of the lining and exterior handles, and press. Pin or baste the turned-under edges.

3. Topstitch around the openings, including both sides of the handles, ⅛″ from the edges. The turned-under edges will be secured in the topstitching.

Pin or baste turned-under edges of handles.

{ elva bag }

{ rebecca bag }

This is a Boston bag that looks like a backpack. It can be made using same-colored fabrics or different fabrics for the handles. The secret to making this a lovely bag is to make sure the front and back pieces are aligned straight when they are sewn onto the zipper panel. This allows the bag to hold its proper form. You can use either home decorator or quilting-weight cotton fabric.

Use the Rebecca Bag Front/Back pattern on pullout page P-3. Use the Rebecca Bag Pocket and the Rebecca Bag Heart (optional) patterns on pullout page P-2.

FINISHED SIZE: approximately
13˝ × 17˝ × 3˝, plus 11˝ handle

SKILL LEVEL: ● ● ●

WHAT YOU NEED

Fabric amounts are based on 44˝-wide fabric.

1-fabric option

  1⅜ yards for exterior

2-fabric option

  1 yard for exterior

  ¾ yard for handles

both options

  1 yard for lining

  ⅜ yard for lining binding (to make your own bias binding, see page 16) OR

  114˝ of ½˝-wide double-fold bias binding (purchased)

  1½ yards of 22˝-wide heavyweight fusible interfacing

  22˝ all-purpose zipper

  10˝ × 7˝ scrap for heart ornament (optional)

  Fiberfill stuffing for heart ornament (optional)

  20˝ of leather cording for heart ornament (optional)

CUTTING THE PIECES

Follow the instructions in Making and Using the Patterns (page 9). Cut the bottom panel, zipper panels, and handles first, and then the remaining pieces. Transfer all points and references to the fabric.

exterior

Cut 1 piece 4″ × 29½″ for the bottom panel.

Cut 2 pieces 2″ × 23″ for the zipper panels.

Cut 4 pieces 3¼″ × 25″ for the handles.

Cut 2 pieces 3½″ × 4″ for the side loops.

Cut 2 Front/Back pieces.

Cut 1 Pocket piece.

lining

Cut 1 piece 4″ × 29½″ for the bottom panel.

Cut 2 pieces 2″ × 23″ for the zipper panels.

Cut 2 Front/Back pieces.

lining bias binding

Refer to Making Bias Binding (page 16) to make 114″ of bias binding, or use purchased binding.

Cut 2 pieces 53″ of bias binding.

Cut 2 pieces 4″ of bias binding.

interfacing

Cut 1 piece 4″ × 29½″ for the bottom panel.

Cut 2 pieces 2″ × 23″ for the zipper panels.

Cut 2 Front/Back pieces.

scrap

Cut 2 Heart pieces.

Preparing the Handles

1. Pin 2 handle pieces together along the 3¼″ edges, with right sides together. Stitch the seam, backtacking at both ends. Press the seam open.

2. Fold in half lengthwise, with the wrong sides together, and press to make a crease. Open the handle with the wrong side facing you. Fold in each side of the handle ½″, and press. Fold in half again along the first crease, and press. Repeat for the remaining 2 handle pieces.

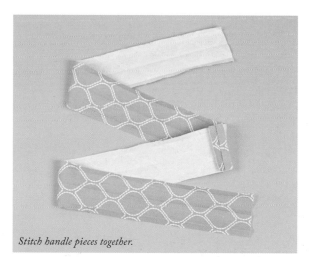

Stitch handle pieces together.

Hem pocket.

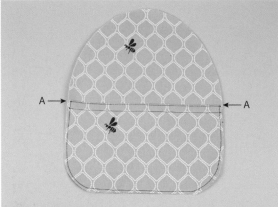

Baste lining, exterior, and pocket together.

Handle lines

Pin handle to exterior from bottom edge to Handle lines.

Attaching the Pocket and Handles

1. To hem the pocket edge, fold over the top (straight) edge of the pocket piece 1″ to the wrong side, and press. Fold over another 1″, and press. Pin and topstitch ⅛″ from both folded edges.

2. Fuse the interfacing to the wrong side of the exterior front, back, zipper, and bottom panels.

3. Pin the exterior front to the lining front, with wrong sides together. Pin the pocket to the exterior front, aligning the side and bottom edges and point A markings. Baste the 3 layers in place.

4. Position a handle over the assembled front, with the 2 ends of the handle aligned with the bottom edges, as indicated on the front/back pattern. Working from the bottom edge upward, pin each side of the handle in place, through all the layers, up to the handle lines. Then pin the remaining folded edges of the handle together.

5. Topstitch both ends of the handle to the assembled front, ⅛″ from the edges. Begin at the bottom edge, and stitch up one side. Pivot at the handle line, and stitch back and forth across the handle line several times to reinforce. Then pivot and continue down the other side of the handle.

6. Topstitch the center portion of the handle between the handle lines, ⅛″ from both long edges, backtacking at the ends.

7. Repeat Steps 3–6 to sew the other handle to the exterior and lining back pieces, omitting the pocket.

Installing the Zipper

1. Referring to the photo at right, close the zipper, and place it on an exterior zipper panel piece, with right sides together. Position the zipper pull ⅝″ from a short end of the zipper panel, and then align the edge of the zipper tape along the top raw edge of the zipper panel. Trim excess zipper tape from the opposite end of the zipper panel, but not closer than ¼″ from the zipper stop. If you need to trim away more of the zipper, see Shortening Zipper Length (page 12).

2. Pin the zipper to the zipper panel.

3. Using a zipper foot, stitch the zipper to the zipper panel, ⅛″ from the edge of the tape, backtacking at both ends.

4. Pin the top edges of the lining zipper panel and the exterior zipper panel with right sides together. The zipper will now be between the top panel and the lining.

5. Using a zipper foot, sew the 3 layers together close to the zipper coils, backtacking at both ends.

6. Flip the lining over to the wrong side, and press. Topstitch the exterior zipper panel close to the zipper coils.

7. Repeat Steps 2–6 to attach the remaining exterior zipper panel and lining zipper panel to the other side of the zipper.

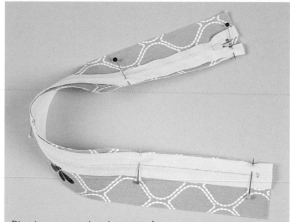

Pin zipper to exterior zipper panel.

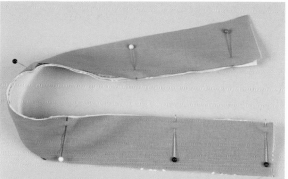

Pin lining zipper panel to exterior zipper panel.

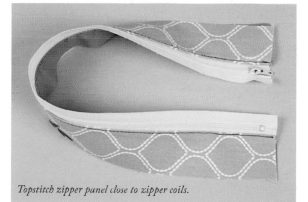

Topstitch zipper panel close to zipper coils.

Attach remaining zipper panels to other side of zipper.

Making the Side Loops

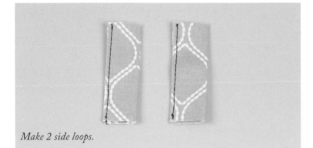

Make 2 side loops.

1. Fold a side loop piece in half lengthwise, with the wrong sides together, and press to make a crease. Open the side loop with the wrong side facing you. Fold in each side of the loop ½″, and press.

2. Fold in half again along the first crease, and press. Topstitch ⅛″ from the folded-in sides. Repeat for the other side loop piece.

Connecting the Zipper Panels and Bottom Panel

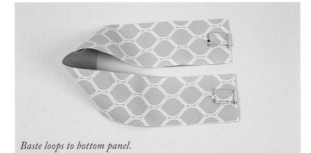

Baste loops to bottom panel.

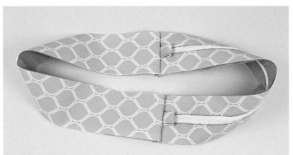

Stitch zipper panel to bottom panel.

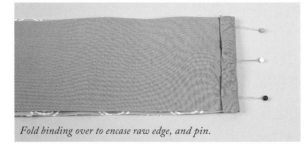

Fold binding over to encase raw edge, and pin.

1. Pin the exterior bottom panel to the lining bottom panel, with wrong sides together, and baste the long edges. Fold the loop pieces in half, and center a folded loop at each short end of the exterior bottom panel, aligning the raw edges. Baste the loops to the bottom panel.

2. Pin the ends of the assembled zipper panel to the ends of the bottom panel to form a ring, with the exterior sides together and the loops sandwiched in between. Stitch the seams. Trim the seam allowances to ⅜″.

3. Unfold a 4″ length of bias binding. Pin the binding to the seam, matching the raw edges, with right sides together.

4. Stitch along the crease line closest to the edge of the seam, backtacking at both ends. Fold the binding over to encase the raw edge, and pin.

5. Topstitch the binding ⅛″ from the inner fold of the binding, through all the layers.

6. Repeat Steps 3–5 for the other seam.

Assembling the Bag

1. Fold the assembled zipper/bottom panel to find and mark the centers of both the zipper panel and the bottom panel. Pin the zipper/bottom panel to the front, with exterior sides together; match the centers to the front centers and the zipper/bottom panel seams to the point B markings on the front. Clip the zipper/bottom panel only as necessary to help ease it around the curve of the front piece.

2. Sew around the bag in 2 sections, stitching from points B to B and backtacking at the end of each section. Trim the seam allowances to ⅜″.

3. Repeat Steps 1 and 2 to attach the back piece.

Adding Bias Binding

1. Unfold the 53″ length of bias binding. Fold and press under a short end of the bias binding ½″. Beginning at the bottom center, pin the raw edge of the bias binding to the outside edge of the bag, with right sides together. Pin all the way around, lapping the end of the bias binding over the folded end ½″.

2. Stitch along the crease line closest to the outside edge. Fold the binding over to encase the raw edge, and pin.

3. Topstitch the binding ⅛″ from the inner fold of the binding, through all the layers. Turn the bag right side out, and press.

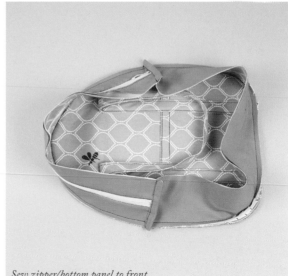

Sew zipper/bottom panel to front.

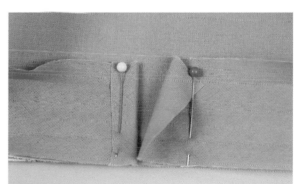

Pin binding around outside edge.

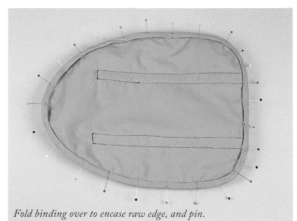

Fold binding over to encase raw edge, and pin.

Making the Heart Ornament

1. Pin the heart pieces, wrong sides together. Sew around the edge using a ½″ seam allowance and leaving 2″ unstitched along the side edge for stuffing. Backtack at the ends.

2. Fill with fiberfill, and stitch the opening closed. Trim the seam using pinking shears.

3. Fold the leather cord in half, and securely sew the ends to the center back of the heart. Loop the folded cord around the handle to attach it to the bag.

Heart ornament

{ rebecca bag }

{ smart school bag }

Have you ever thought about carrying your own handmade bag to school? Well, now you can! The various pockets inside the bag make it possible to store a variety of things, from pencil cases to papers. Durable canvas, corduroy, recycled denim, or thick linen fabric work especially well for this bag, and you won't have to interface it!

Use the Smart Schoolbag Bottom Corner and the Smart Schoolbag Flap Corner patterns on pullout page P-2.

FINISHED SIZE: 17″ × 14″, plus 28″ handle

SKILL LEVEL: ●●

WHAT YOU NEED

> *Fabric amounts are based on 44″-wide fabric.*
>
> 1⅛ yards for exterior
>
> 1⅛ yards for lining
>
> 8″ of 1″-wide hook-and-loop tape
>
> 1½″–2½″ toggle or button (optional)

CUTTING THE PIECES

Follow the instructions in Making and Using the Patterns (page 9). Transfer all points and references to the fabric.

exterior

Cut 2 pieces 18″ × 44″ for the front and back. Refer to the Bag diagram to mark the pieces and to trace and trim the bottom corners using the Smart Schoolbag Bottom Corner template. Use the measurements on the Bag diagram and the Smart Schoolbag Flap template to trim out a large rectangle on each piece, forming the straps. Save a large piece that you cut away to use for the flap.

From the large piece that you saved when cutting the front and back, cut 1 piece 13½″ × 13″ for the flap. Refer to the Flap diagram to mark the piece and to trace and trim the bottom corners using the Smart Schoolbag Flap Corner template.

lining

Cut 2 pieces 18″ × 44″ for the front and back. Refer to the Bag diagram to mark the pieces and to trace and trim the bottom corners using the Smart Schoolbag Bottom Corner and the Smart Schoolbag Flap Corner templates. Save the large pieces that you cut away to use for the flap and the pocket.

From a large piece that you saved when cutting the front and back, cut 1 piece 13½″ × 13″ for the flap. Refer to the Flap diagram to mark the piece and to trace and trim the bottom corners using the Smart Schoolbag Flap Corner template.

From the remaining saved pieces, cut 2 pieces 13″ × 7″ for the pocket.

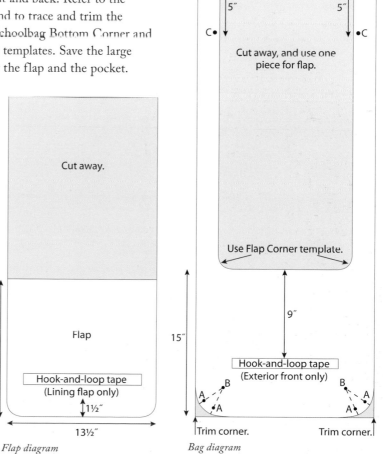

Flap diagram

Bag diagram

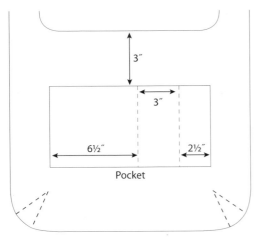

3″

3″

6½″   2½″

Pocket

Pocket Placement diagram

Making the Pocket

1. Make the pocket (see Making a Pocket, page 14). Refer to the Pocket Placement diagram to center the pocket on the right side of a lining front or back piece, with the upper (12″ finished) edge of the pocket placed 3″ from the top edge of the lining. Topstitch the pocket in place—down one side, across the bottom, and back up the other side, backtacking at both ends.

2. To separate the pocket into smaller sections, stitch a seam 6½″ from the left edge of the pocket, backtacking at the ends to secure. Stitch another seam 2½″ from the right edge in the same manner.

Sew front and back darts, and press.

Sewing the Exterior and Lining

1. Separate the hook-and-loop tape, and attach the softer piece to the exterior front as marked. Sew the rougher half to the lining flap as marked.

2. Sew the darts on the exterior front and back pieces (see Sewing Darts and Pleats, page 16). Press the darts on the front piece toward the center and on the back piece toward the outside seams.

3. Pin the exterior front and back pieces together around the outside edge, from the top of one handle to the top of the other, with right sides facing. The darts on the front and back pieces will be pressed in opposite directions, so they will lie flat.

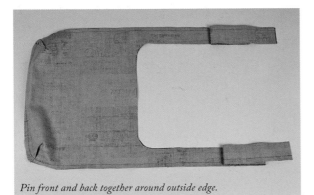

Pin front and back together around outside edge.

4. Sew around the outside edge, backtacking at both ends. Notch the curved seam. Press the seam open.

5. Repeat Steps 2–4 with the lining pieces, leaving 5″ unstitched along the bottom edge for turning.

Assembling the Exterior and Lining

1. Turn the exterior right side out. Insert the exterior inside the lining, with right sides together.

2. Pin the exterior and lining together around the inner curved seams on both the front and back between the C markings (see Bag diagram, page 137).

3. Stitch the inner curved seams as pinned on both the front and the back, backtacking at both ends. Clip the curved seams. Turn the bag right side out through the opening left in the lining. Push out the handles. Slipstitch the opening closed.

4. Pin the short edges of the exterior handles together, right sides facing.

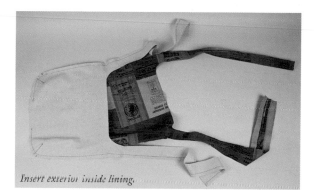

Insert exterior inside lining.

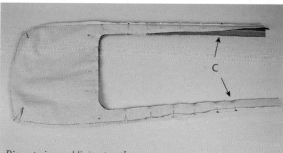

Pin exterior and lining together.

Pin short edges of exterior handle together.

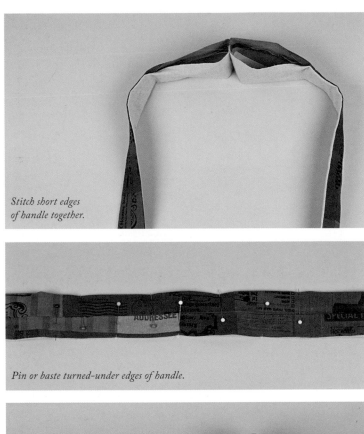

Stitch short edges of handle together.

Pin or baste turned-under edges of handle.

Topstitch around handle.

5. Stitch the seam, backtacking at both ends. Press the seam open. Repeat for the lining handle.

6. Turn under ½″ on the raw side edges of the lining and exterior handle, and press. Pin or baste the turned-under edges.

7. Topstitch around the handle and the top of the bag, ⅛″ from the edges. The turned-under edges will be secured in the topstitching.

Attaching the Flap

1. Optional: If you are attaching a toggle, center the cords on the right side of the curved edge of the exterior flap. Stitch in position ⅜″ from the edge, backstitching to secure.

2. Pin the exterior flap and lining flap, with right sides together. Stitch around the flap, leaving 3″ unstitched on the top straight edge for turning. Trim the corners, and notch the curved seam. Trim the seam allowance to ¼″.

3. Turn right side out. Press, and topstitch ⅛″ from the outer curved seam only. Tuck in the seam allowances on the unstitched opening, press, and slipstitch the opening closed.

4. Center the flap on the back of the bag, 1″ down from the top edge. Pin the flap to the bag. Check the position of the hook-and-loop tape and adjust the flap if needed. Stitch in place along the straight edge, backtacking at both ends to reinforce.

5. Optional: Sew the button in place.

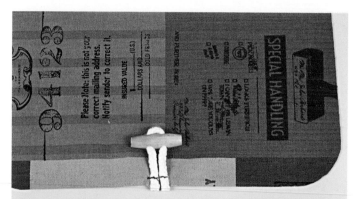

Attach optional toggle.

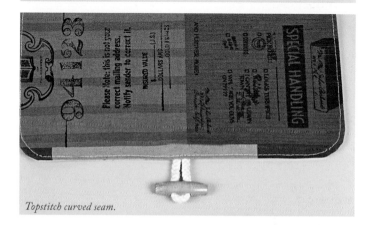

Topstitch curved seam.

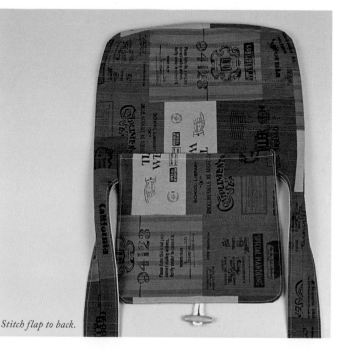

Stitch flap to back.

Bags—The Modern Classics

{ about the author }

Sue Kim lives in Toronto with her three lovely children and husband. Currently she is running the PDF pattern website ithinksew.com. Her projects will help you have fun as you gain confidence and experience. Sue has a keen eye for style and a special talent for making fashionable and functional clutches and bags.

Resources

beingbags.etsy.com
beingbags@yahoo.com
San Jose, CA

Amy Butler Design
122 South Prospect Street
Granville, OH 43023
amybutler.design.com
Tel.: 740-587-2841
Fax: 740-587-2842

Michelle Dunn
www.kallistiquilts.com
www.kallistiquilts.etsy.com
Tel.: 519-569-8718

Evelyn's Sewing Centre
17817 Leslie Street, Unit 40,
Newmarket, ON L3Y 8C6, Canada
thequiltstore.ca
Tel.: 905-853-7001

Fabricland
fabricland.ca
fabriclandwest.com

Robert Kaufman Fabrics
Box 59266, Greenmead Station
Los Angeles, CA 90059
info@robertkaufman.com
Tel.: 310-538-3482
Toll-Free: 800-877-2066

Miami Leather Company
Box 131
Morden, MB R6M 1V9, Canada
Tel.: 204-435-2878 Ext. 282

Michael Miller Fabrics, LLC
118 West 22nd Street, 5th Floor
New York, NY 10011
info@michaelmillerfabric.com
Tel.: 212-704-0774
Fax: 212-633-0272

mimis.etsy.com
6533 County Highway 27
Springville, AL 35146
Tel.: 205-467-7565

stashBOOKS

fabric arts for a handmade lifestyle

If you're craving beautiful authenticity in a time of mass-production...Stash Books is for you. Stash Books is a line of how-to books celebrating fabric arts for a handmade lifestyle. Backed by C&T Publishing's solid reputation for quality, Stash Books will inspire you with contemporary designs, clear and simple instructions, and engaging photography.

www.stashbooks.com